THE UNOFFICIAL HOCUS POCUS COOKBOOK

Bewitchingly Delicious Recipes
for Fans of the Halloween Classic

BRIDGET THORESON

ULYSSES PRESS

Published by:
ULYSSES PRESS
PO Box 3440
Berkeley, CA 94703
www.ulyssespress.com

ISBN: 978-1-64604-241-8
Library of Congress Control Number: 2021937731

Printed in China
10 9 8 7 6 5

Acquisitions editor: Ashten Evans
Managing editor: Claire Chun
Editor: Kate St.Clair
Proofreader: Renee Rutledge
Front cover design: Chelsea Hunter
Interior design and layout: what!design @ whatweb.com
Artwork: shutterstock.com except pages 12, 18, 26, 40, 44, 58, 65, 66, 69, 70, 72, 82, 86, 96, 100, 102, 109, 114, 138 © Bridget Thoreson

To '90s Kids, and '90s Kids at Heart

Contents

Introduction

Hocus Pocus first premiered 28 years ago in the golden age of '90s cinema (can you believe it was that long?). You may remember the time—high school was a horror, kids from California were all laid-back surfer dudes, and parents were always impossibly out of touch and uncool, despite firm clues that, perhaps, they actually weren't.

Despite these extremely time-bound tropes, *Hocus Pocus*, unlike the Sanderson sisters and likely most of us, hasn't aged. Okay, it has, but overall it has aged fairly well. Outside a few insensitive teenager remarks, the story and script are every bit as enjoyable today as they were nearly 30 years ago.

Perhaps it is for that reason that the movie seems to have so many more fans today than in the 1990s. When the movie first premiered, it was not a resounding success. However, over time, more and more people came to know the film, appreciating its wholehearted '90s-ness, its camp, or its ability to be both grisly and pure.

Like its substory, *Hocus Pocus* is getting better with age, and each year draws new devoted fans. Which is why it seems to make perfect sense to write a fan book now, three decades "late." This book is a celebration of *Hocus Pocus*, its characters, and of course, its big musical number for no apparent reason (seriously, how could Bette Midler singing "I Put a Spell on You" not have clinched a Grammy and an immediately thriving fan base from the get-go?). The cookbook format draws inspiration from Winifred's unholy spellbook, and the recipes pay tribute to fan-favorite moments, characters, and lines from the movie. One recipe even comes from the dialogue itself, though it moves so fast in parts, you might miss it!

I hope you enjoy this homage to *Hocus Pocus* as much as you enjoy the film itself. While blondies are no substitute for Bette and no cocktail is quite as funny as hearing a young girl humiliate her older brother by saying "Yabos," I hope you'll find the recipes and references fun, delicious, and delightfully spooky, and you'll rewatch the film again and again accompanied by the goodies in this booo-ooooo-ooook.

Now, preheat your cauldron, pick a treat, and get ready for some culinary *magic*.

Brooms, ho!

TOOLS FOR YOUR "TORTURE CHAMBER"

Baking rack	Double boiler	Parchment paper
Blender	Immersion blender	Paring knife
Cast-iron skillet	Mason jars	Pastry brush
Chef's knife	Matches	Potato masher
Cocktail shaker	Meat tenderizer	Strainer
Colander	Measuring cups	Wax paper bags
Cutting board	Muffin tin	Wire whisk
Dutch oven		

Life-Giving Fall Favorites

A SPELL FOR CINNAMON BREAD

One dark fall eve when the moon is round,
Enjoy this cinnamon bread so nicely browned.
With butter and sugar and a dash of spice,
Even Master himself can't resist a slice.

SERVES: 8 | PREP TIME: 15 MINUTES | COOK TIME: 50 MINUTES

2 cups all-purpose flour

1 cup plus 2 tablespoons white sugar, divided

2 teaspoons baking powder

½ teaspoon baking soda

2½ teaspoons ground cinnamon, divided

1 teaspoon salt

1 cup buttermilk

¼ cup vegetable oil

2 eggs

2 teaspoons vanilla extract

2 teaspoons unsalted butter

1. Preheat the oven to 350°F and grease a 9 x 5-inch loaf pan.

2. Mix the flour, 1 cup of the sugar, baking powder, baking soda, 1½ teaspoons cinnamon, salt, buttermilk, oil, eggs, and vanilla in a large bowl, and beat for about 3 minutes until well combined. Pour into the loaf pan and smooth the top.

3. Combine the remaining sugar, cinnamon, and butter until crumbly. Sprinkle over the top of the batter in the loaf pan.

4. Bake for about 50 minutes, or until a toothpick inserted into the middle comes out clean.

HEARTY BREAKFAST FRITTATA

You never know what any day might bring. For instance, you might wake up one morning thinking it will be just another day in the new town you just moved to—only to, in the course of 24 hours, get publicly burned by a girl who later becomes your girlfriend, have your kicks stolen, ignite ancient witchcraft, raise the dead, accidentally cause every adult in town to be ensnared in a magic dancing spell, and stay up the whole night trying to figure out how to outsmart a coven of witches.

I think it goes without saying, then, that it's important to fuel up at breakfast and start every day with your best foot forward—just in case. This frittata is the perfect addition to a hearty breakfast. Add a side of fresh fruit and you'll be ready to tackle just about anything life—or death—might throw at you.

SERVES: 8 | PREP TIME: 15 MINUTES | COOK TIME: 25 MINUTES

6 eggs
3 tablespoons heavy cream or half-and-half
2 tablespoons olive oil
6 ounces grated cheddar cheese
¾ cup chopped white onion

¾ cup chopped zucchini
¾ cup chopped tomato
2 tablespoons unsalted butter
salt and freshly ground pepper, to taste

1. Preheat the oven to 425°F.

2. Whip together the eggs, cream or half-and-half, salt, and pepper with a wire whisk. Stir in the cheddar cheese.

3. Heat the skillet on the stove over medium-high heat. Add the olive oil.

4. Sauté the onion until soft, about 5 minutes. Then add the zucchini and sauté for 2 to 3 minutes. Add the tomato and butter, and finish sautéing the vegetables so that they are all cooked through.

5. Pour the egg and cheese mixture over the sautéed vegetables and let them cook on the stove for about 1 minute.

6. Transfer the skillet to the oven and let the frittata bake for 8 to 15 minutes, or until the edges are golden brown. Remove the frittata from the oven and let it sit for 2 to 3 minutes before cutting into it.

AUTUMNAL PUMPKIN BREAD

While modern Halloween may have been "invented" by the candy companies, Mars, Hershey, and friends don't have a monopoly on fall flavors. Autumn is the time for pumpkin, squash, cinnamon, and other spices to really shine, and numerous fall flavors delight in this enchanting pumpkin bread.

SERVES: 12 | PREP TIME: 15 MINUTES | COOK TIME: 65 MINUTES

butter to grease the loaf pans

2 cups all-purpose flour, plus more to sprinkle on the loaf pan

½ teaspoon salt

1 teaspoon baking soda

½ teaspoon baking powder

1 teaspoon ground cloves

1 teaspoon ground cinnamon

1 teaspoon ground nutmeg

¼ teaspoon ground ginger

1½ sticks unsalted butter, softened

2 cups sugar

2 large eggs

1 (15-ounce) can pumpkin puree

½ cup roasted pumpkin seeds (optional)

1. Preheat the oven to 325°F.

2. Grease two 8 x 4-inch loaf pans with butter and then sprinkle with flour.

3. Add the flour, salt, baking soda, baking powder, cloves, cinnamon, nutmeg, and ginger to a medium bowl. Blend the dry ingredients together well with a wire whisk.

4. In a separate bowl, add the softened butter and sugar. Beat the butter and sugar mixture with a hand mixer until blended. Add an egg and beat until blended, and then add the second egg. Blend in the pumpkin puree until fully combined and fluffy.

5. Add the flour mixture and beat with the mixer until fully combined. If using, fold in the pumpkin seeds by hand.

6. Split the batter between the two greased pans.

7. Bake for approximately 65 minutes, and remove from the oven when a cake tester inserted into the center of the bread comes out clean.

8. Let the bread set for 10 minutes then transfer to a cooling rack to finish cooling to room temperature.

PUMPKIN PANCAKES

))))﴾﴾﴿﴿ᴄᴄᴄᴄ

If the thought of having a glorious morning doesn't make you sick, here's the perfect way to start the day. These healthy pumpkin pancakes are not only delicious, they're autumnally festive and chock-full of good ingredients.

SERVES: 10 │ PREP TIME: 10 MINUTES │ COOK TIME: 10 MINUTES

2 cups all-purpose flour

3 teaspoons baking powder

1 teaspoon salt

1½ teaspoons ground cinnamon

½ teaspoon ground ginger

1 teaspoon ground nutmeg

¼ cup (½ stick) unsalted butter

¼ cup granulated sugar

¼ cup brown sugar

1 teaspoon vanilla extract

1 cup pumpkin puree

2 large eggs

1½ cups whole milk

1. Add the flour, baking powder, salt, cinnamon, ginger, and nutmeg to a large bowl. Blend the ingredients well with a wire whisk.

2. Melt the butter on the stove over medium heat, or in the microwave.

3. Add the sugar, brown sugar, vanilla, pumpkin puree, eggs, melted butter, and milk to a separate bowl. Mix well with a wire whisk.

4. Add the pumpkin mixture to the flour mixture and whip together with a large fork. You want to leave the mixture a bit lumpy; do not let it get completely smooth.

5. Let the batter sit for approximately 10 minutes.

6. Heat a griddle or nonstick pan over medium heat. Spray with nonstick spray or add butter and let it melt.

7. Pour approximately ¼ cup of batter per pancake onto the griddle in circles. When the top of the pancake starts to bubble, flip the pancake.

8. Remove when fully cooked and serve.

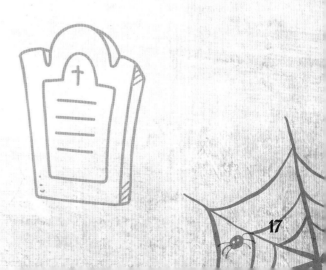

APPLE PORK CHOPS

If you feel the icy breath of death upon your neck, I'm sorry to say, you might soon turn to dust. But if it's simply the chill of an autumn wind sneaking 'neath your scarf, you may just be saved. These hearty chops are sure to fill your belly and warm your soul, warding off any potentially grim guests.

SERVES: 2 | PREP TIME: 10 MINUTES | COOK TIME: 25 MINUTES

2 pork chops

4 tablespoons (½ stick) unsalted butter, divided

2 Gala apples, cored and sliced

10 ounces apple butter, divided

2 tablespoons dark brown sugar

1 teaspoon chili powder

⅓ cup half-and-half

salt

freshly ground pepper

1. Season the pork chops with salt and pepper.

2. Heat a cast-iron skillet over high heat.

3. Add 2 tablespoons of butter to the skillet.

4. When the butter is melted, sear the pork chops so they are browned on both sides. Transfer the pork chops to a plate and set aside.

5. In the same skillet add the remaining 2 tablespoons of butter and the sliced apples. Cook the apples over medium heat until they start to soften.

6. Add 6 ounces of apple butter, the brown sugar, and the chili powder to the skillet and blend them with the apples.

7. Pour in the half-and-half and stir. Bring the sauce to a simmer.

8. Once the sauce begins to simmer, make space in the center of the skillet by moving the apples aside. Then add the pork chops back to the skillet so that they sit flush against the bottom of the skillet.

9. Glaze the top of the pork chops with more apple butter and cook for about 4 minutes. Then flip the pork chops and glaze with more apple butter.

10. Plate the pork chops and top them with the apple slices and apple butter mixture.

BLACK MAGIC BEEF STEW

If All Hallows' Eve in your town has been overtaken by little brats running amok, or if a lot of spooky things seem to happen, or if it's simply a full moon when the weirdos are out, feel free to stay inside and spend a quiet evening at home. Keep yourself company through the witching hour with a cozy book of spells, a cup or two of Newt Saliva (page 98), and a hearty bowl of this delicious stew.

SERVES: 8 | PREP TIME: 20 MINUTES |
COOK TIME: 4 HOURS, 45 MINUTES TO 8 HOURS, 45 MINUTES

3 sprigs fresh rosemary
3 sprigs fresh thyme
2 bay leaves
2 pounds beef stew meat
4 tablespoons olive oil
6 carrots, cut into 1½-inch pieces
1 white onion, diced
3 cloves garlic, thinly sliced

1 pound quartered red potatoes
1 teaspoon smoked paprika
3 tablespoons tomato paste
4¼ cups beef stock, divided
¼ cup all-purpose flour
2 tablespoons fresh parsley leaves (optional)
sea salt
freshly ground pepper

1. Using cooking twine, bundle and tie the rosemary, thyme, and bay leaves.

2. Season the beef generously with sea salt and pepper.

3. Heat a cast-iron skillet on the stove on high heat. When the skillet is hot, lower to medium heat and add the olive oil. Give the oil approximately 2 minutes to heat up.

4. Add the beef to the skillet and brown it on all sides. Remove from the heat.

5. Add the beef, carrots, onion, garlic, potatoes, and paprika to a slow cooker.

6. Add the tomato paste and 4 cups of beef stock and stir well. (Add more beef stock or water if necessary to make sure the beef, potatoes, and vegetables are covered.)

7. Add the bundled herbs to the stew so that they are submerged in the beef stock.

8. Cover and cook on low for 7 to 8 hours or on high for 3 to 4 hours.

9. Remove the bundle of herbs.

10. In a small bowl, whisk together the flour and ¼ cup of beef stock so that the flour is completely dissolved.

11. Stir the flour and broth mixture into the stew then cover and cook on high for another 30 minutes.

12. Garnish with parsley, if using, and serve.

CHICKEN POT PIE

If you're one of the lucky ones who went out trick-or-treating and made it home without waking the undead or nearly getting your soul sucked out, congratulations—you made good choices. Make another one and warm up from the frosty New England night air with this delicious chicken pot pie.

SERVES: 8 | PREP TIME: 20 MINUTES | COOK TIME: 50 MINUTES

2 large chicken breasts

2 pie crusts (page 127) or store-bought pie crusts

½ cup butter (1 stick)

1 onion, diced

⅓ cup flour

1¾ cups chicken stock

½ cup milk

1½ (12-ounce) bags or 1 (18-ounce) bag frozen mixed vegetables (corn, carrots, and peas)

salt

freshly ground pepper

garlic powder

1. Heat the oven to 400°F.

2. Season the chicken breasts with salt, pepper, and garlic powder.

3. Bake the chicken on a greased baking sheet until it reaches 160°F (approximately 20 minutes).

4. Remove the chicken and increase the oven temperature to 425°F.

5. Cut the chicken into small chunks and set aside.

6. Roll out the pie crust and place it in a pie plate.

7. Heat the butter in a large saucepan over medium heat.

8. When the butter is melted, add the onion and sauté until cooked through.

9. Lower the heat and add the flour, salt, and pepper, and mix it until completely blended.

10. Bring the stove back up to medium heat, add the chicken stock and milk, and stir until it starts to simmer. Let it simmer until it starts to thicken.

11. Add the chicken and the mixed vegetables, and mix well.

12. Remove the filling from the heat and scoop into the pie crust.

13. Roll out the top of the pie crust. Lay it over the pie and fold the edges underneath the bottom crust.

14. Use a fork to imprint the edges of the crust and to poke holes in the top of the crust so it can breathe while it bakes.

15. Cover the edges of the crust with aluminum foil and place the pie in the middle of the oven.

16. Let the pie bake for approximately 20 minutes and then remove the foil.

17. Let the pie bake for approximately 15 minutes, or until the pie is properly browned.

18. Let the pie cool for 10 minutes before cutting into it and serving.

FRENCH ONION SOUP

The fiery leaves, the crisp cool air, breaking out your fiercest red cape—there's nothing like fall in New England. As Daylight Saving Time draws to a close and the dark of night stretches longer in each direction, you'll need hearty, rib-sticking meals to warm your belly, your hands, and your soul on spooky Salem evenings. This French Onion Soup is just the ticket.

SERVES: 6 | PREP TIME: 5 MINUTES | COOK TIME: 30 MINUTES

6 tablespoons butter
3 large sweet onions, thinly sliced
3 cloves garlic, thinly sliced
2 tablespoons flour
⅔ cup red wine
4 cups beef stock

8 sprigs fresh thyme
1 bay leaf
1 baguette
1 cup grated gruyère cheese
sea salt
freshly ground pepper

1. In a Dutch oven, melt the butter over medium heat. Add the onions and toss them in the butter until they are golden brown.

2. Add the garlic and continue to toss in the butter until fragrant.

3. Add the flour and stir until fully blended with the butter and onions.

4. Season with the salt and pepper.

5. Add the red wine and deglaze the Dutch oven, scraping all of the browned bits from the bottom.

6. Bring the red wine and onions to a simmer and let it sit for approximately 3 minutes.

7. Tie the fresh thyme and bay leaves into a bundle with cooking twine.

8. Add the beef stock and the fresh herbs. Bring to a slow boil and then let it simmer for 15 to 20 minutes.

9. Remove the herbs and season with salt and pepper. Turn off the heat.

10. Slice the baguette diagonally into 1-inch slices.

11. Ladle the soup into oven-safe ramekins. Place a baguette slice on top and sprinkle a desired amount of grated cheese on top.

12. Broil on high until the cheese is bubbling.

13. Remove from the heat and serve.

MAC 'N' CHEESE

Cheese and crust, you'll lose your head for this tasty dish! It's almost wicked how sinfully delicious these few simple ingredients can be. Macaroni and cheese is never *not* the perfect meal choice, but on a cool autumn night when the breeze is rustling through the trees and the sky is black, a comfort dish like this is nothing short of marvelous.

SERVES: 8 | PREP TIME: 15 MINUTES | COOK TIME: 60 MINUTES

1 pound large-shell pasta

1 tablespoon olive oil

10 ounces grated extra-sharp cheddar cheese, divided

8 ounces grated gruyère cheese, divided

½ cup all-purpose flour

½ cup (1 stick) plus 4 tablespoons unsalted butter, divided

3 cups half-and-half

⅓ cup seasoned bread crumbs

salt

freshly ground pepper

1. Preheat the oven to 350°F.

2. Bring a large pot of salted water to boil.

3. Add the pasta and cook so that it is al dente, per the package directions.

4. Drain the pasta in a colander and pour it into a 12-inch cast-iron skillet.

5. Add the olive oil to the pasta, toss, and set aside.

6. Combine the cheddar and gruyère cheeses and set aside.

7. In a saucepan, melt ½ cup of unsalted butter over medium heat.

8. Add the flour to the butter and whisk well until fully combined.

9. Add the half-and-half and whisk well. Continue whisking until it simmers.

10. Lower the heat to low and add the cheese in batches, mixing well so that it fully melts. Continue adding the cheese until approximately ⅓ is left.

11. Pour the cheese mixture over the pasta and mix well.

12. Sprinkle the bread crumbs over the top of the pasta.

13. Cut the remaining 4 tablespoons of butter into thin slices and place them on the top of the pasta.

14. Sprinkle the remaining cheese over the pasta.

15. Bake the pasta for approximately 20 minutes, or until the top of the cheese is melted and slightly browned.

SQUASH RAVIOLI

)))))((((·

Even if most of his actions are positively brainless, our brave little virgin does have one thing right—there *is* something more powerful than magic, and it is knowledge. Knowledge of time zones can help you escape witches, knowledge of 1950s blues hits can help you entrance a crowd, and knowledge of how to make homemade pasta can help you impress and enchant your guests.

SERVES: 6 | PREP TIME: 3 HOURS | COOK TIME: 30 MINUTES

2 cups diced butternut squash

6 cloves garlic, divided

½ cup diced white onion

1 tablespoon olive oil

1 tablespoon brown sugar

4 ounces grated parmesan cheese, divided

Homemade Pasta (page 128)

½ cup (1 stick) unsalted butter

2 rosemary sprigs

⅛ cup bread crumbs

salt

freshly ground pepper

RAVIOLI FILLING

1. Preheat the oven to 425°F.

2. In a medium-sized bowl, toss the squash, half the minced garlic, and diced onion with olive oil, brown sugar, salt, and pepper.

3. Place the squash mixture on a greased baking sheet and bake for approximately 30 minutes.

4. Remove from the oven and let it cool for 5 minutes.

5. Add to a food processor with 2 ounces of cheese and pulse until fully pureed.

PASTA

1. Roll out the Homemade Pasta (see page 128).

2. Once the dough is rolled out, place a large round glass, about 2 to 3 inches in diameter, rim-side down on the dough. Use the glass as a stencil and cut circles out of the dough with a paring knife.

3. Place a dollop of the squash puree on the center of each circle of dough and then fold the dough in half, pinching the edges together.

4. Let the ravioli sit out for 20 minutes to set.

5. Bring a large pot of well-salted water to boil.

6. Add the ravioli and cook for approximately 3 minutes, stirring occasionally.

7. Remove ⅛ cup of pasta water and set aside.

8. Drain the water from the ravioli in a colander.

SAUCE

1. Brown the butter per the instructions on page 83; set aside the foamed butter from the process.

2. When the butter starts to brown, add the remaining garlic and rosemary sprigs. Keep the rosemary somewhat together so it can be easily removed.

3. Sauté the garlic in the browning butter. Before the garlic is finished, add ⅛ cup of pasta water.

4. Remove the butter from the heat before the garlic turns dark brown. Add the foamed butter you removed earlier in the process. You may also add olive oil if you'd prefer more sauce for the ravioli. Remove the rosemary sprigs.

5. In a large bowl sprinkle the ravioli with bread crumbs. Pour the brown butter sauce over the ravioli, and toss.

6. Plate the ravioli and sprinkle with the remaining grated cheese.

PUMPKIN SOUP

What *can't* a good pumpkin do? In everything from pancakes to pies, everyone's favorite fall squash shines from morning 'til night. This stick-to-your-ribs soup is just another example of its flexibility. Thick, warm, and hearty, it's perfect for fattening up a small child or just enjoying on its own.

SERVES: 4 | PREP TIME: 10 MINUTES | COOK TIME: 50 MINUTES

1 (4-pound) pumpkin
1 tablespoon extra-virgin olive oil
1 large white onion, diced
4 cloves garlic, diced
4 cups chicken stock

½ cup heavy cream
sea salt
freshly ground pepper
roasted pumpkin seeds, for garnish

1. Cut the pumpkin in half and scoop out the seeds. Peel the skin from the pumpkin and cut the flesh into chunks.

2. Heat the olive oil in a Dutch oven over medium heat. Add the onion and sauté until fragrant, about 5 minutes. Then add the garlic and continue to sauté until it is golden brown and fragrant.

3. Add the pumpkin chunks and pour the chicken stock over them. Add salt and pepper to taste. Bring the soup to a boil, reduce the heat, and simmer for about 30 minutes. The pumpkin should be tender when stabbed with a fork.

4. Remove the soup from the heat and blend with an immersion blender until it is smooth and creamy.

5. Whisk in the heavy cream and add roasted pumpkin seeds to garnish. Serve warm.

BRIDGET BISHOP'S BAKED APPLES

The real Salem witch trials began in the spring of 1692, more than a year before our story begins. The first woman executed for being a witch was Bridget Bishop, an eccentric Englishwoman who married thrice (scandalous!).

Whether she was actually a witch or simply "a singular character, not easily described," as Charles Upham wrote (and which would almost certainly have been seen as a crime itself in Puritanical Massachusetts), we may never know.

The citizens of Salem in the 17th century likely had simple tastes and would not enjoy most desserts in this book, but I think "Goody" Bishop might've enjoyed these delicious baked apples.

SERVES: 10 | PREP TIME: 10 MINUTES | COOK TIME: 25 MINUTES

2 Granny Smith apples, cored and sliced
4 Fuji apples, cored and sliced
2 tablespoons unsalted butter
3 tablespoons honey
1 tablespoon cornstarch

3 teaspoons ground cinnamon
¼ teaspoon ground cloves
¼ teaspoon sea salt
2 tablespoons bourbon
vanilla ice cream, to serve

1. Heat the oven to 350°F.

2. Peel the apple slices (optional) and place them in a mixing bowl.

3. Melt the butter and pour it over the apples.

4. Add the honey, cornstarch, cinnamon, ground cloves, sea salt, and bourbon, and toss well.

5. Place the apple mixture into a baking dish and bake until the apples are tender. Stab the apples with a fork to check their tenderness, and remove from the oven before they get mushy.

6. Serve the apples with vanilla ice cream.

CARAMEL APPLES

If you're not into bullying and you already know how to breathe through your nose, why not use your afternoon to whip up these spine-chillingly sweet caramel apples? A classic fall treat, you can keep these plain and simple or dress them up with your leftover Halloween candy.

The traditional way to make caramel apples is to insert a stick near the stem and dip the whole apple. That's lovely but can get messy, so you can also try cutting the apples into slices and dipping bite-sized pieces.

SERVES: 8 | PREP TIME: 10 MINUTES | COOK TIME: 40 MINUTES

8 tart apples
1 cup (2 sticks) unsalted butter
2 cups packed brown sugar
1 cup light corn syrup

1 (14-ounce) can sweetened condensed milk
2 teaspoons vanilla extract
toppings such as sprinkles, candies, mini marshmallows, or chopped nuts (optional)

1. Wash and prepare your apples. You can dip whole apples in boiling water and dry with a paper towel if the skins feel waxy after washing. Remove the stems and push a chopstick into the top of the apple like a lollipop or cut the apples into slices for easier eating. Line a baking sheet with parchment paper.

2. In a medium saucepan stir together the butter, brown sugar, corn syrup, and condensed milk over medium-high heat. Bring to a boil while stirring constantly and then lower the heat to medium.

3. Cook, stirring constantly for 25 to 30 minutes, or until a candy thermometer reads 248°F. At this point, drop a small bit of caramel into a glass of cold water—it should form a small, firm ball. Remove from the heat and stir in the vanilla extract.

4. Quickly dip each apple or slice into the caramel as high as you like, but not more than ½ inch from the top.

5. Place on the parchment paper, decorate with toppings if you wish, and let cool.

PUMPKIN PIE

You haven't really been to hell until you've been to high school, as our three spooky spinsters quickly learn. While actual hell may be quite lovely, we all know high school is just a temporary prison for children. If you've had a tough time at school, or just a day that feels as difficult as high school was, treat yourself to an afternoon snack. A slice of this pumpkin pie is just the trick (or treat) you'll need for comfort.

SERVES: 8 | PREP TIME: 10 MINUTES | COOK TIME: 50 MINUTES

1 pie crust (page 127) or store-bought pie crust
3 large eggs
1 (15-ounce) can pumpkin puree
1 cup light brown sugar
1 tablespoon all-purpose flour

½ teaspoon salt
1 teaspoon ground cinnamon
1 teaspoon ground ginger
½ teaspoon ground nutmeg
⅛ teaspoon ground cloves
1 (12-ounce) can evaporated milk

1. Preheat the oven to 425°F.

2. Line a pie plate with the pie crust. Set aside.

3. Beat the eggs in a small bowl.

4. Combine the pumpkin puree, brown sugar, flour, salt, cinnamon, ginger, nutmeg, cloves, beaten eggs, and evaporated milk in a large bowl. Whisk until completely blended.

5. Pour the pie filling into the pie crust.

6. Place the pie in the middle of the oven and bake for 15 minutes.

7. Reduce the heat to 350°F and bake for 35 more minutes. If the crust appears to be baking too quickly, use foil to cover the edges of the pie crust.

8. Remove from the oven and set it out to cool before serving.

Recipes for Salem Townsfolk

BAKED WITCH CASSEROLE

Should thou find thyself in a battle of wits against three witches or tackling a complicated recipe, you shall require the appropriate tools. A pottery kiln may leave the former unscathed, while proving overkill on the latter. For this simple and tasty baked casserole, a run-of-the-mill kitchen oven shall serve thee well enough.

SERVES: 8 | PREP TIME: 15 MINUTES | COOK TIME: 1 HOUR

1½ pounds russet potatoes, peeled and diced

½ cup heavy cream

5 tablespoons unsalted butter

1½ teaspoons kosher salt, divided

3 cloves garlic, minced, divided

2 tablespoons olive oil

1 medium white onion, diced

½ cup diced celery

¾ cup chopped green bell pepper

2 pounds ground beef

1 cup crushed tomatoes

⅔ cup seasoned bread crumbs

1½ tablespoons Worcestershire sauce

1½ tablespoons tomato paste

fresh parsley, for garnish

1. Preheat the oven to 400°F.

2. Place the potatoes in a pot and fill with water until they are covered. Bring the water to a boil on high heat. Reduce the heat to keep the water simmering. Allow the potatoes to cook for approximately 15 minutes, until they are tender. (Test the potatoes by stabbing them with a fork.)

3. Drain the water when the potatoes are cooked.

4. Add the heavy cream, butter, 1 teaspoon of kosher salt, and 1 clove of minced garlic. Mash the potatoes until they are smooth and the ingredients are well blended.

5. Place a cast-iron skillet on the stove and heat it on high. Just before the skillet starts to smoke, add the remaining garlic, olive oil, onion, celery, and bell pepper, and sauté until they are soft.

6. Add the ground beef and sauté until it is cooked.

7. Remove from the heat and add the remaining salt, crushed tomatoes, bread crumbs, Worcestershire sauce, and tomato paste. Mix the sauce into the ground beef filling.

8. Spread the meat filling into a casserole dish or the cast-iron skillet. Spread the mashed potatoes evenly over the meat filling. Place the casserole in the middle of the oven and let it bake for 25 minutes.

9. Garnish with parsley.

ROASTED PUMPKIN SEEDS POWER SNACK

No matter whether you're a growing teenager or a 300-year-old cat, your energy will flag during a long night of dodging witches. Keep your spirits and blood sugar up with these roasted pumpkin seeds. This savory snack is sure to receive the stamp of approval from mangy felines and virgins alike.

(Just kidding, seeds aren't actually recommended for cats, but if you're immortal and cursed either way, you might want to try them.)

SERVES: 12 | PREP TIME: 20 MINUTES (40 MINUTES IF YOU DECIDE TO CARVE A JACK-O'-LANTERN) | COOK TIME: 15 MINUTES

1 (5-pound) pumpkin
½ teaspoon salt
¼ teaspoon garlic powder

¼ teaspoon paprika
⅛ teaspoon freshly ground pepper
1 tablespoon olive or avocado oil

1. Cut a circle on the top of the pumpkin around the stem and remove the top.

2. With a large metal spoon, scoop the seeds and pulp out of the pumpkin into a colander.

3. Use a marker to draw a face on the front of the pumpkin and then cut out the face with a serrated knife. Place the pumpkin on the front stoop with a lit candle inside.

4. Place the colander of pulp and seeds in the sink and rinse off the pulp. It's alright if some pulp remains.

5. Preheat the oven to 350°F.

6. Pour the seeds onto a layer of paper towels and then dab the seeds with more paper towels. Allow the seeds to sit for 10 minutes to dry. While they dry, whisk together the salt, garlic powder, paprika, and pepper.

7. Pour the seeds into a mixing bowl and drizzle them with the oil.

8. Sprinkle the seeds with seasoning and mix the seeds until they are evenly coated.

9. Spread the seeds out on a baking sheet and bake them in the oven for 12 to 15 minutes. While they are baking, toss the seeds with a spatula every few minutes so they do not stick to the baking sheet.

10. Transfer the seeds to a bowl and serve.

MISCHIEF NIGHT PASTA

))))の(((

Traditionally, "mischief night" is supposed to be the night before Halloween, but if you're a teen boy in the '90s who is interested in mischief night, you're probably not that interested in rules anyway, so might as well get into trouble on Halloween, too. Please, keep your mischief on the tame side—TP'ing the neighbor's house, harassing children, and being rude to women are not endearing behaviors, and no one will be upset if they wind up getting you locked in a cage, toyed with, and nearly eaten. That'd be a fitting punishment, many would say.

SERVES: 6 | PREP TIME: 10 MINUTES | COOK TIME: 30 MINUTES

*Homemade Pasta (page 128),
cut into ½-inch-wide strips*

2 pounds ground sausage

2 heads broccoli, cut into medium-sized florets

½ cup (1 stick) unsalted butter

2 teaspoons minced garlic

1½ cups heavy cream

2 cups freshly grated pecorino romano cheese

½ teaspoon salt, plus an extra pinch for the water

¼ teaspoon pepper

fresh parsley, for garnish

1. Bring a large pot of salted water to a boil and add the pasta.

2. Cook the pasta (if you haven't already) for approximately 3 minutes, stirring constantly. (You may want to have a small piece of the pasta, separate from the sheets in the water, so you can taste a small piece to test if it is cooked.)

3. Drain the pasta and set aside.

4. Sauté the sausage over medium heat until browned. Set aside.

5. Steam the broccoli in a steamer pot for 5 minutes. Set aside.

6. To make the alfredo sauce, melt the butter in a medium skillet over medium heat.

7. Add the garlic to the skillet before the butter is completely melted.

8. Add the cream to the skillet, then add salt and pepper. Whisk continuously until the cream starts to simmer.

9. Add the cheese a bit at a time, whisking regularly until it's fully melted.

10. Add the pasta, sausage, and broccoli to a large bowl. Pour in the cheese and gently toss to combine.

11. Plate and serve.

WITCHES' HAIR PASTA

I wouldn't exactly call the townsfolk of Salem innocent—they're a little too into all this Halloween stuff, they're not exactly friendly and welcoming, and many of them are likely descended from possible witch hunters and at least probable puritanical prudes. But that doesn't mean they deserve to be enslaved to dance until they die and have their small children gobbled up by a gaggle of witches. Luckily, as is often the case with adults in kids' movies, they are largely oblivious to just how close they came to a tragic end. I'm happy for them. It's not their fault a laid-back California airhead virgin moved to town and decided to run amok.

If the townsfolk *did* realize the peril they were in, they may have less-than-fond memories of a certain town hall party and surprise concert appearance. In fact, some may be inclined toward revenge and take a page out of a witch's unholy book and cook up this spinster spaghetti.

SERVES: 4 | PREP TIME: 20 MINUTES | COOK TIME: 3½ HOURS

2 sprigs fresh thyme

2 sprigs fresh rosemary

2 bay leaves

4 plum tomatoes

4 vine tomatoes

½ can tomato paste

2 pounds rump roast (or beef chuck)

4 tablespoons olive oil, divided

1 large white onion, diced

4 cloves garlic, thinly sliced

4 medium celery stalks, diced

4 medium carrots, diced

1 cup red wine

¾ cup beef stock

1 (16-ounce) box spaghetti

shredded pecorino romano cheese

salt

freshly ground pepper

1. Bind the fresh thyme, rosemary sprigs, and bay leaves with cooking twine.

2. Core the plum tomatoes and vine tomatoes. Place them in a blender with the tomato paste and blend well.

3. Cut the beef into 3 to 4 large pieces. Pat it dry and season it with the salt and pepper.

4. Heat 2 tablespoons of olive oil in the Dutch oven over high heat.

5. Add the beef and brown it on all sides. Remove the beef and set it aside on a plate.

6. Add the remaining olive oil and reduce the heat to medium.

7. Add the onion and sauté for 2 to 3 minutes.

8. Add the garlic and continue to sauté until fragrant, without burning.

9. Add the celery and carrots and continue to sauté for 5 to 7 minutes.

10. Return the beef to the pot. Add the tomatoes, wine, and beef stock, and mix well until fully blended.

11. Plunge the bound herbs into the sauce. Increase the heat and continue to stir until the sauce begins to simmer.

12. Once the sauce begins to simmer, reduce the heat so that it continues to slowly bubble.

13. Cover the pot, leaving a slight opening on the edge, and allow the sauce to simmer for 2 hours. Stir occasionally.

14. Remove the beef from the pot and place on a cutting board. Using two large forks, shred the beef. Return the shredded beef to the pot and allow the sauce to simmer for another 30 to 40 minutes.

15. Add more salt and pepper to taste.

16. While the shredded beef and sauce are simmering, bring a large pot of salted water to boil.

17. Once the water is boiling, add your favorite pasta and cook according to the package directions. (If you prefer to make you own pasta, see the recipe on page 128.)

18. Serve the sauce over the pasta, topped with the shredded pecorino romano cheese.

SALTY SWEET CARAMEL CORN

·)))◗◖(((·

If you want to conjure up the most popular Halloween party in town, you simply must have the most demonically delicious snacks. There's no need to sell your soul for the secret to this crowd-pleasing caramel corn, I'll tell you right now: it's a lot of brown sugar and an extra pinch of salt—just to be safe.

SERVES: 12 | PREP TIME: 5 MINUTES | COOK TIME: 1½ HOURS

2 tablespoons vegetable oil

7 quarts popped popcorn (approximately 1 cup of unpopped kernels)

1 cup (2 sticks) unsalted butter

½ cup corn syrup

2 cups packed light brown sugar

¼ teaspoon cream of tartar

1 teaspoon salt

1 teaspoon baking soda

1 teaspoon vanilla extract

1. Heat the vegetable oil in a large wok or pot over medium heat.

2. While the vegetable oil is heating, place three unpopped kernels in the bottom and cover with a lid.

3. When the kernels pop, add the remaining kernels, cover, and remove from the heat.

4. Hold the pot or wok with the lid on tight and gently shake it away from the heat for approximately 30 seconds.

5. When the kernels start to pop, return them to the medium heat.

6. As the kernels continue to pop, lift the pot and gently shake it to keep kernels from remaining stationary on the bottom and burning.

7. When the kernels appear to be popped, or the sound of the popping reduces to fewer than three pops per second, turn off the heat,

remove the pan, and keep shaking until the popping stops completely.

8. When the popping stops, quickly pour the popped kernels into a bowl.

9. Mix the butter, corn syrup, and brown sugar in a medium saucepan. Bring to boil over medium high heat. Once bubbling, let boil for 6 minutes.

10. Remove from the heat and add the cream of tartar, salt, baking soda, and vanilla extract. Stir until the mixture becomes creamy. Preheat the oven to 200°F.

11. Pour the mixture over the popcorn and mix until well coated. Spread the coated popcorn over 2 or 3 buttered or greased baking sheets (depending on size) or rectangular cake pans. Bake for 1 hour at 200°F, stirring halfway through.

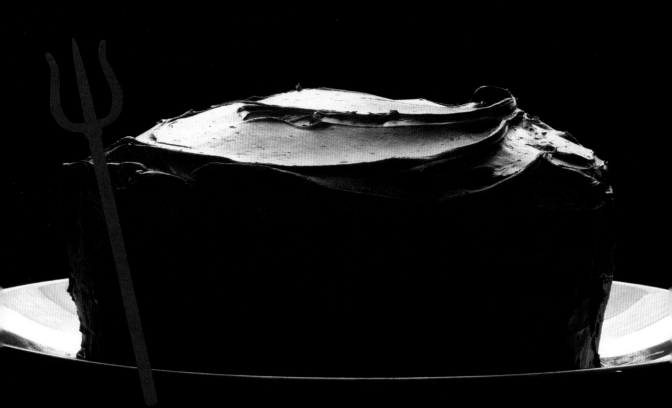

MASTER'S DEVIL'S FOOD CAKE

)))) • ((((

Not every witch is sufficiently wicked to meet Master in the flesh. If thou art not one of his chosen few, fear not. Conjure up this demonically decadent devil's food cake in his honor. With ganache of chocolate darker than the still of night, it is sure to ensnare the senses in unholy temptation.

SERVES: 8 | PREP TIME: 25 MINUTES | COOK TIME: 25 MINUTES

¾ cup (6 ounces) unsalted butter, softened

1½ cups granulated sugar

2 large eggs

2 cups all-purpose flour, plus more for dusting pans

½ cup unsweetened cocoa powder

½ teaspoon baking soda

½ teaspoon salt

½ cup hot water

½ cup whole milk

1 teaspoon vanilla extract

Chocolate Buttercream (see below)

1. Preheat the oven to 350° F. Coat two 9-inch round cake pans with nonstick spray, or with grease and flour (depending on your preferred method).

2. In a medium bowl, beat the butter with a mixer on medium speed until light and fluffy. Add the sugar and beat again until fluffy (about 3 minutes).

3. Add the eggs one at a time, beating well after each.

4. Stir together the flour, cocoa powder, baking soda, and salt in a bowl. Add bit by bit to the butter mixture, alternating with the hot water and milk, and beating after each portion is added. You should start and end with the flour mixture.

5. Stir in the vanilla.

6. Pour evenly into the two cake pans and bake for 20 to 25 minutes, until a toothpick inserted in the middle comes out clean. Let cool completely before frosting with the Chocolate Buttercream.

CHOCOLATE BUTTERCREAM

½ cup (1 stick) room temperature unsalted butter or margarine
½ cup solid vegetable shortening
¾ cup unsweetened cocoa powder

1 teaspoon vanilla extract
4 cups sifted powdered sugar
3 to 4 tablespoons milk

1. In a large bowl, cream the butter and shortening together with a mixer on medium speed. Add in the cocoa powder and vanilla, mixing and scraping the sides of the bowl until all ingredients are incorporated.

2. Add in the powdered sugar 1 cup at a time and mix after each portion. Scrape the bowl often to incorporate. Drizzle in the milk, and mix until the icing is light and fluffy.

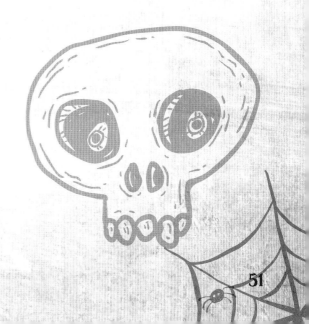

CHOCOLATE WITCH POPS

A classic snack for every party thrown in the '90s, the chocolate lollipop is the perfect nostalgic treat. These can be marvelously simple to make, but are just as easily dressed up with colored white chocolate or candy decorations. Most recipes call for simple chocolate meltables from the local craft store—but for a slightly elevated version, feel free to buy higher quality chocolate.

If only real-life witches could be dispatched as easily and quickly as these are—a simple bite of the head and your ghoulish tormentors would be but dust.

SERVES: 8 | PREP TIME: 10 MINUTES | COOK TIME: 10 MINUTES, PLUS 40 MINUTES TO SET

1 (12-ounce) bag semisweet chocolate chips
1 teaspoon vegetable oil

2 ounces baker's wax
witch-shaped molds
wooden craft sticks

1. Heat the chocolate in a double boiler so that it melts, stirring continuously.

2. As the chocolate begins to melt, add the vegetable oil and baker's wax and continue to stir until fully melted. It is best to have the chocolate at approximately 90°F.

3. Pour the chocolate into witch-shaped molds.

4. Stick the craft sticks into the mold, cover with wax paper, and refrigerate for 40 minutes.

5. Remove carefully from the mold and store in a sealable plastic bag in the refrigerator.

DUMP OUT YOUR CHOCOLATE SACK

Inspired by the candy toll raucous teenagers often impose on younger trick-or-treaters, this take on the chocolate bag ice cream sundae is sure to delight—but hopefully not overwhelm—your stomach. Use any candy you want, but no licorice. I recommend a chocolate peanut butter or chocolate mint palate, personally. Whatever you choose, just be sure not to "pig out." (Just kidding, eat what you want, I don't support food shaming; but teenagers in the '90s were a different story.)

SERVES: 4 | PREP TIME: 30 MINUTES | CHILL TIME: 4 HOURS

8 ounces dark chocolate morsels
raspberry sauce
caramel sauce
ice cream

candies, your choice, for toppings
fruit, your choice, for toppings
whipped cream

1. Use a wax paper bag that is rectangular in shape when opened. Ideally the bag will be approximately 3-inches wide and 6-inches tall.

2. Fold down the bag to create a 2-inch lip. This will leave about 4 inches in height for the bag, and the lip will be used to handle the bag once the chocolate is inside it.

3. Heat the chocolate in a double boiler so that it melts. It is best to have the chocolate at approximately 90°F.

4. Using a pastry brush, brush the chocolate to the inside of the bags. Apply 2 coatings to the sides and then brush the bottom with the chocolate that drips down.

5. Place the bags in the freezer for at least 4 hours.

6. When ready, gently tear the paper from the outside of the bags until all that is left is the chocolate bag.

7. Once the bags are frozen, you can move them to the refrigerator if you intend to serve them within 3 hours.

8. When you are ready to serve, garnish a plate with raspberry and caramel sauce to create a decorative setting.

9. Place the bag lying down in the middle of the plate.

10. Scoop ice cream into the bag so that it appears to be spilling out of the bag.

11. Decorate the bag and ice cream with your selected candy (and/or fruit) so that it looks like the candy spilled out over the plate.

12. Top with whipped cream and more raspberry or caramel sauce as desired.

GINGERBREAD WITCHES' HOUSE

You might think gingerbread houses are for Christmas, but with the right candy decorations, this cookie cottage can be spooky enough for any witch in the woods to spend a quiet evening at home. Whether you use bread crumbs or song to lure children to your gate, they won't be able to resist this charming candy cabin.

SERVES: 6 | PREP TIME: 3½ HOURS | COOK TIME: 12 MINUTES

3 cups all-purpose flour
1 teaspoon baking soda
1 teaspoon ground cinnamon
¾ teaspoon ground ginger
½ teaspoon ground allspice
½ teaspoon ground cloves
½ teaspoon salt
¼ teaspoon freshly ground pepper

½ cup (1 stick) unsalted butter at room temperature
¼ cup vegetable shortening at room temperature
½ cup light brown sugar
⅔ cup molasses (unsulfured)
1 large egg
1 teaspoon vanilla extract
assorted candies, and canned or tubed frosting, for decorating

1. Preheat the oven to 350°F and position the racks so that one is in the top third of the oven and the other is in the bottom third.

2. Sift the flour, baking soda, cinnamon, ginger, allspice, cloves, salt, and pepper through a wire mesh sieve into a medium bowl.

3. Combine the butter and shortening in a large bowl with a hand mixer. Mix on high until it is well blended.

4. Add the brown sugar and mix with the hand mixer. Then add the molasses, egg, and vanilla extract and mix again with the hand mixer.

5. Gradually add in the flour mixture and mix it with a wooden spoon to make a firm dough.

6. Divide the dough in half and cover it with plastic wrap. Refrigerate for 3 hours.

7. Remove half the dough from the refrigerator and bring to room temperature.

8. Spread flour on the countertop. Use a rolling pin to roll out the dough so that it is approximately ⅛-inch thick. (The thinner you roll out the dough, the crunchier and harder the cookies will be.)

9. Cut the dough into desired shapes to construct the gingerbread house. You can combine and refrigerate the scraps before rolling them out again to cut more cookies. Repeat with the remaining half of the dough.

10. Bake the cookies for 10 to 12 minutes, swapping the racks halfway through.

11. Let cool completely, then use frosting and candies to construct your house however you please.

POPCORN BALLS

)))●(((

Remember the disappointment of trick or treating and receiving a homemade popcorn ball instead of candy? Well, we can't all be the house that gives out a jackpot of king-size chocolate bars, though I wouldn't recommend passing out homemade treats these days. But for a nice nostalgic Halloween party snack, popcorn balls can't be beat. Easy to make, easy to nibble and, best of all, younger witches are in no danger of crashing out on too much sugar.

SERVES: 20 | PREP TIME: 10 MINUTES | COOK TIME: 10 MINUTES

5 quarts popped popcorn (approximately ⅔ cup of unpopped kernels)

2 tablespoons vegetable oil

¾ cup corn syrup

¼ cup margarine

2 teaspoons cold water

2½ cups powdered sugar

1 cup marshmallows

1 cup candy corn (optional)

1 tablespoon vegetable shortening

1. Pop the popcorn per the instructions on page 48 using the vegetable oil.

2. Combine the corn syrup, margarine, cold water, powdered sugar, and marshmallows in a small saucepan.

3. Heat over medium heat, stirring regularly until the marshmallows are melted and the mixture is fully combined.

4. In a large bowl, combine the marshmallow mixture and popcorn using a rubber spatula so that all of the kernels are coated. If you would like to add candy corn, mix it in now.

5. Coat hands with the vegetable shortening and then form the popcorn into balls, placing each ball on wax paper.

6. Cover the popcorn balls with plastic wrap and store at room temperature.

CLEVER LITTLE WHITE (WITCH) CHOCOLATE CHUNK COOKIES

How many witches make an appearance in *Hocus Pocus*? Three we know for sure, of course. But our favorite coven identifies a potential fourth. Could our teen queen truly be the clever white witch they claim she is?

On the one hand, she's extra curious to get into the book of spells, she's super into witches and she knows a lot of witch lore. On the other hand, she comes from a wealthy Salem family, which means they're probably descended from real witch hunters, isn't aware of the secret of salt, and doesn't see the book's magical glow. The jury's still out on this teenage witch; but in the meantime, here's a clever little recipe for white witch chocolate chunk cookies!

SERVES: 8 | PREP TIME: 15 MINUTES | COOK TIME: 12 MINUTES

1 cup packed brown sugar

½ cup granulated sugar

1 cup unsalted butter, softened

1 teaspoon vanilla extract

2 eggs

2½ cups all-purpose flour

1 teaspoon baking soda

½ teaspoon baking powder

1 teaspoon salt

¼ teaspoon ground cinnamon

1 (11-ounce) bag white chocolate chips

1. In a large bowl, mix together the brown sugar, granulated sugar, softened butter, and vanilla extract. Beat with a mixer on medium speed for about 2 minutes until fluffy.

2. Add in both eggs and beat until fully combined.

3. In a medium bowl, mix together the flour, baking soda, baking powder, salt, and cinnamon. Add slowly to the wet ingredients with the mixer on low until combined.

4. Mix in the white chocolate chips by hand. Cover well and refrigerate for at least 35 minutes.

5. Allow the dough to come to room temperature so you can spoon it onto sheets. Preheat the oven to 350°F and line the baking sheets with parchment paper or nonstick spray.

6. Spoon the dough onto the baking sheets, about 1 to 1½ tablespoons at a time.

7. Bake in the oven for approximately 12 minutes until lightly golden. Cool and serve or store.

TUNA BISCUIT DINNER FOR A VERY HELPFUL CAT

After 300 years of constant vigilance, even the most fiercely independent of cats deserves a rest. A loving family, warm bed, and a little home-cooked meal may be simple, but likely sounds divine to a mangy feline.

This simple tuna dinner is an easy way to show your cat how much you love and appreciate all they've done for you—and perhaps for many children and families over the years. Feel free to serve it with milk every day, so they turn into one of those fat house cats and only need to hunt mice for fun.

SERVES: 6 | PREP TIME: 10 MINUTES | COOK TIME: 10 MINUTES

2 cups canned, low-sodium tuna

4 eggs

¼ cup vegetable oil

4 cups bread crumbs

1. Preheat the oven to 350°F.

2. Open the canned tuna and fully drain it.

3. Beat the eggs in a small bowl.

4. Combine the tuna, eggs, vegetable oil, and bread crumbs in a medium bowl and mix well with a fork.

5. Scoop the mixture onto a greased baking sheet in approximately ¼ cup portions.

6. Bake for 10 minutes.

7. Serve with milk.

From the Witches' Spellbook

A LITTLE CHILD...ON TOAST

))))◦(((

Plotting eternal youth and taking care of a cheating boyfriend certainly doesn't leave much time for mothering. If things had turned out differently, perhaps a little child of a witch's own would have been quite nice. Imagine cozy days over the cauldron, cavorting with her aunts. But...'twas not the life you chose, and now instead you may have your little child on toast! Perhaps with some fruit jam to sweeten up her little rat face and rotten attitude.

SERVES: 1 | PREP TIME: 2 MINUTES | COOK TIME: 5 MINUTES

1 slice sourdough bread
½ tablespoon salted butter, softened
cooking spray

1 egg
salt
freshly ground pepper

1. Cut a hole out of the middle of the sourdough bread, approximately 1½ inches in diameter.

2. Spread the butter on both sides of the bread.

3. Heat a frying pan over medium heat.

4. Spray the pan with cooking spray, return it to the heat, and then add the slice of bread.

5. Break the egg so that it falls into the center of the slice of bread.

6. Cook the egg and toast until the bottom of the toast is browned, and then flip the egg and toast together.

7. Add salt and pepper while the egg and toast finish cooking.

8. Remove the egg and toast from the heat when the toast finishes browning.

BONES OF 100 CHICKENS

)))))0(((((

Is it a bit macabre to make references to eating children? Yes, of course. But these witches like what they like and have a sniffer finely tuned to wee babes. Like them, you won't be able to resist the spicy smell of these hot wings, though I don't recommend using the leftover bones to build your front gate.

SERVES: 2 | PREP TIME: 10 MINUTES | COOK TIME: 40 MINUTES

2 tablespoons salted butter
12 small chicken wings
1 tablespoon olive oil
2 tablespoons hot sauce

2 tablespoons Old Bay seasoning
1 tablespoon Cajun seasoning
1 tablespoon garlic powder

1. Preheat the oven to 425°F.

2. Melt the butter in a microwave.

3. Add the chicken wings to a mixing bowl and pour the olive oil, butter, and hot sauce over them. Mix well so they are all coated.

4. Add the Old Bay, Cajun seasoning, and garlic powder. Mix well so the wings are all coated.

5. Place the wings on a greased baking sheet.

6. Bake for 40 minutes, or until browned and crispy.

DEAD MAN'S TOES, DEAD MAN'S TOES

))}◗◍◖(((

Alas, it's so difficult to find a good dead man's toe these days, never mind keeping it fresh once you do. Though it certainly is easier than it was 300 years ago before the marvelous little invention called a refrigerator. The ancestors of today's witches really were cursed with so many more struggles—how to keep potion ingredients fresh, how to hide their devilry from small-minded townsfolk in a tiny village, how to stay young and beautiful without the aid of retinol. But necessity truly is the mother of invention. And speaking of invention, with a good supply of dead man's toes, you can conjure almost anything—including a hellishly spooky party. These appetizers are marvelously macabre. But if you're interested in a less revolting refreshment, keep the mustard on the side and the hot dogs uncut.

SERVES: 8 | PREP TIME: 15 MINUTES | COOK TIME: 12 MINUTES

8 hot dogs
1 package Pillsbury crescent rolls

1 tablespoon ketchup
1 tablespoon your favorite kind of mustard

1. Preheat the oven to 375°F.

2. Cut the hot dogs into equal halves.

3. Open the crescent rolls container. Unroll the dough and cut it so that you have 16 similarly sized triangles.

4. Roll each hot dog half with a crescent roll so that the cut half of the hot dog is wrapped in the dough and the uncut half is sticking out fully exposed.

5. Using a sharp paring knife, make two or three thin shallow slits in the top of the hot dog toward the middle right at the edge of the crescent roll dough (this will be the knuckle).

6. On the top of the hot dog at the uncut edge, use the paring knife to cut half of a long ellipse out of the top of the hot dog so that it looks like the shape of a fingernail bed.

7. Place the hot dog rolls on a greased baking sheet and bake for approximately 12 minutes.

8. When the hot dog rolls are done, use a pastry brush or small spoon to cover the nail bed of the hot dogs with the mustard or ketchup.

Variation: For a fancier manicure, you can make a mustard glaze by heating ¼ cup Dijon mustard, ⅛ cup Worcestershire sauce, and ⅛ cup light brown sugar in a small saucepan over medium heat until the ingredients melt together and thicken. Brush on the nail beds before the hot dog buns go in the oven.

LIFE POTION SOUP

You don't need an enchanted song, a decent singing voice, or even the Devil's own book to make this next recipe. Just as you don't need to suck the lives out of little children to stay healthy and strong—this life potion soup gives you a nice big serving of vegetables that will help keep you looking young...well, younger.

An important tip to remember: the more zucchini lives you snatch, the longer you shall live—I mean, eat. (This recipe is easily doubled for more leftovers so you can share with your fool sisters, or hoard it all for yourself.) So fire up that medium-sized cauldron and you'll have this recipe bubbling in two shakes of a lucky rat's tail.

SERVES: 6 | PREP TIME: 10 MINUTES | COOK TIME: 35 MINUTES

4 medium zucchini, shredded with a cheese grater
1 medium white onion, thinly sliced
½ cup salted butter
2½ cups chicken broth
¼ cup packed fresh basil leaves

1 cup heavy cream
½ teaspoon ground nutmeg
sea salt
freshly ground pepper

1. In a Dutch oven, sauté the zucchini and onion in the butter until the onion is fragrant.

2. Add the broth, salt, and pepper and stir. Bring to a boil and let it simmer for 15 to 20 minutes.

3. Remove from the heat and let it sit for 5 minutes to cool.

4. Add the basil.

5. Use an immersion blender and blend the ingredients until completely smooth.

6. Add the heavy cream and nutmeg and stir well.

7. Season again with salt and pepper to taste.

8. Return to heat and bring to a soft boil. Reduce the heat and simmer until it is heated to desired temperature to serve.

A SPELL FOR FLAYED AND CRISPY BREAST OF CHICKEN

·)))⟩✺◗❋◖(((·

Twist the meat and pound it flat,
Trim it of the chicken fat.
Salt and pepper, black as black,
Then cook like this...

SERVES: 6 | PREP TIME: 30 MINUTES | COOK TIME: 20 MINUTES

3 boneless chicken breasts
3 cups flour
4 eggs
3 cups seasoned bread crumbs
¼ cup grated parmesan cheese

1 tablespoon garlic powder
1 teaspoon salt
½ teaspoon freshly ground pepper
olive oil

1. Preheat the oven to 425°F.

2. Flay each chicken breast.

3. Using a meat tenderizer, tenderize each flayed breast to desired thinness.

4. Scoop the flour into a bowl.

5. Whip the eggs in a separate bowl.

6. Blend the bread crumbs, parmesan cheese, garlic powder, salt, and pepper in a separate bowl.

7. Pat each chicken breast dry.

8. One by one, dredge each chicken breast in the flour, shake off excess flour, then dunk in the egg, dredge in the bread crumbs, and then set aside.

9. On a baking sheet, generously drizzle olive oil. Place each chicken breast directly on the olive oil. Then, drizzle more olive oil, generously on the tops of the chicken breasts.

10. Cook in the oven for 10 minutes, and then flip the chicken breasts.

11. Cook for another 10 minutes.

DEAD MAN'S CHUNGS

I won't speak for any man, but when it comes to body parts they'd give up for a witch's potion, I'm sure many would gladly volunteer a toe or a nose if it meant they could hang onto their chungs. Happily, this recipe isn't quite so hair-raising and no men—dead or undead—are required to achieve a most bewitching dish.

SERVES: 4 | PREP TIME: 20 MINUTES, PLUS 30 MINUTES TO CHILL | COOK TIME: 20 MINUTES

REMOULADE SAUCE

4 medium green onions, chopped

1 clove garlic, chopped

1 cup mayonnaise

¼ cup chili sauce

2 tablespoons Creole mustard

2 tablespoons extra-virgin olive oil

1 tablespoon Louisiana-style chili pepper hot sauce

2 tablespoons fresh lemon juice

1 teaspoon Worcestershire sauce

2 tablespoons chopped fresh parsley

½ teaspoon Cajun seasoning

1 teaspoon salt

½ teaspoon freshly ground pepper

1 teaspoon Old Bay seasoning

CRAB CAKES

1 pound lump crabmeat
⅓ sleeve lightly salted crackers
1 egg
¼ cup mayonnaise

2 green onions, finely chopped
2 teaspoons Old Bay seasoning
olive oil

1. Add all remoulade ingredients to a medium mixing bowl and blend well with a rubber spatula. Set aside.

2. Gently separate the crab meat and check for shells without breaking up the lumps of crab meat.

3. Crush the crackers in a sealed bag so that they are completely crushed, while leaving some slightly larger pieces.

4. Beat the egg in a small bowl.

5. In a large mixing bowl, add the crab meat, crackers, mayo, green onions, egg, and Old Bay seasoning.

6. Gently mix the ingredients with a rubber spatula so that they are well blended, without breaking the large lumps of crab meat.

7. Refrigerate for 30 minutes.

8. Preheat the oven to 350°F.

9. Remove the crab meat mixture from the refrigerator and gently press it into small balls, approximately the size of a ping-pong ball.

10. Drizzle some olive oil onto a baking sheet and place the crab cakes on the sheet in the oil.

11. Bake the crab cakes for approximately 10 minutes so they are warm all the way through.

12. Finish the crab cakes by broiling for approximately 2 to 3 minutes (watch them closely so they do not burn).

13. Place the crab cakes on a serving platter with a small ramekin of the remoulade sauce for dunking.

I SMELL SCROD!

Despite its ghoulish name and spine-tingling status as a bottom-dweller, scrod is actually a very tasty fish—a small cod or haddock, in fact. Technically you don't even need a recipe for this dish, as it's right there in the movie itself: just add some lovely bread crumbs and margarine, or even olive oil is good and, behold! A lovely flaky white fish dinner.

SERVES: 4 | PREP TIME: 5 MINUTES | COOK TIME: 20 MINUTES

3 tablespoons margarine
2 cloves garlic, minced
1 cup panko bread crumbs
olive oil
4 fillets of scrod (cod or other white fish)

2 tablespoons lemon juice
1 teaspoon sea salt
fresh parsley
lemon wedges

1. Preheat the oven to 400°F.

2. Melt the margarine in a small skillet over medium heat.

3. When the margarine is melted, add the garlic and sauté until it is lightly brown and fragrant.

4. Add the panko bread crumbs and sauté until they are browned and the margarine is absorbed.

5. Remove the bread crumbs from the heat and stir in the sea salt. Place the mixture in a small bowl and set aside.

6. Generously drizzle olive oil onto a baking sheet.

7. Place the scrod directly on the olive oil so that it does not stick to the pan when it cooks.

8. Lightly drizzle olive oil on the top of the scrod.

9. Gently pack the breadcrumb mixture on the top of the scrod.

10. Spritz the tops of the scrod with lemon juice.

11. Bake for 10 to 15 minutes until the scrod is white and cooked through.

12. Plate the scrod with parsley garnish and lemon wedges.

BLOOD OF OWL SOUP

Mix this blood of owl (tomato) soup with some herb that's red (red pepper flakes), add some sourdough croutons, and you'll conjure up a sinfully delicious elixir worthy of any wicked witch's evil spellbook.

SERVES: 6 | PREP TIME: 10 MINUTES | COOK TIME: 40 MINUTES

6 cups chopped vine tomatoes
1 white onion, diced
2 cloves garlic
2 teaspoons dry basil
2 cups chicken stock
2 teaspoons sea salt
1 tablespoon honey

2 teaspoons white sugar, to taste
red pepper flakes, to taste
2 tablespoons salted butter
2 tablespoons all-purpose flour
¼ cup heavy cream
fresh basil, for garnish

1. Combine the tomatoes, onion, garlic, dry basil, chicken broth, sea salt, honey, sugar, and red pepper flakes in a large stock pot.

2. Heat over medium heat, stirring occasionally until it boils.

3. Reduce heat to a gentle boil for approximately 20 minutes.

4. Remove from the heat and blend well with an immersion blender.

5. In another pot, heat the butter and flour on medium heat. Mix it continuously until it is smooth and golden brown.

6. Slowly pour in the tomato broth, stirring constantly with a whisk to make sure there are no lumps.

7. Add the cream and blend with the whisk.

8. Continue to heat until the soup is at a desired temperature.

9. Season to taste with salt and/or sugar.

10. Garnish with fresh basil.

SHUSH KE-BABY KEBABS

)))❂(((

If you're having a very special guest for dinner—or perhaps a whole townful, if you're lucky—these kebabs are sure to hit the spot. They're perfect for oven or grill cooking, easily prepped ahead of time if you're entertaining, and supernaturally easy to clean up.

SERVES: 6 | PREP TIME: 10 MINUTES | COOK TIME: 15 MINUTES

2 pounds beef steak (sirloin or tenderloin)	2 fresh rosemary sprigs
1 red bell pepper	2 fresh thyme sprigs
1 tomato	sea salt
1 yellow squash	freshly ground pepper
1 red onion	garlic powder
olive oil	onion powder
3 cloves garlic	steak sauce or melted butter (optional)

1. Cut the steak into 1-inch pieces.

2. Cut the pepper, tomato, squash, and onion into thick slices large enough to be skewered.

3. Season the steak with sea salt and pepper.

4. Preheat the grill to 400°F.

5. Once the steak has rested, skewer the steak and vegetables on a metal skewer.

6. Season the skewers with sea salt, pepper, garlic powder, and onion powder.

7. Grill the skewers, flipping halfway through, until charred on the outside.

8. Optional: As the skewers cook on the grill, glaze with your favorite steak sauce or melted butter.

Options for Cooking the Steak:

· **Sous vide:** Place the steak in a vacuum-sealed bag with garlic cloves, rosemary, thyme, and 6 tablespoons salted butter. Submerge in a bucket of water and cook at 128°F with the sous vide for approximately 2 hours. Finish on the grill over high heat to achieve a charred finish.

· **Stove top:** Heat a cast-iron skillet on high heat. When the skillet is hot, add olive oil. Add the steak to the skillet with halved garlic cloves, rosemary, thyme, and 2 tablespoons of butter. Remove the steak from the pan and let it rest for 10 minutes.

Steak and Potatoes Variation: For a heartier kebab, add some potatoes to the mix. To prep the potatoes for use, preheat the oven to 400°F. Cut 5 pounds of Yukon Gold potatoes into thick slices. Add to a sheet pan, drizzle olive oil, and season with sea salt, garlic powder, onion powder, and pepper. Bake for approximately 40 minutes, so that they are almost fully cooked but still a bit too firm. Cool before using for your skewers.

GINGER-DEAD MEN

Unfaithful lovers who once were dead,
Will love this substitute for gingerbread.
Measure and knead and flour and roll,
Twist thy fingers into the dough.
These treats are sweet, this I know, and quickly shall these cookies go!

SERVES: 24 COOKIES | PREP TIME: 1½ HOURS, INCLUDING CHILL TIME | COOK TIME: 10 MINUTES

3 cups all-purpose flour
1 teaspoon baking powder
½ teaspoon salt
1 cup unsalted butter, softened

1 cup sugar
1 tablespoon milk
1 large egg
1 teaspoon vanilla extract

1. Add the flour, baking powder, and salt to a large bowl. Whisk until well blended.

2. Add the butter and sugar to another large bowl. Using a hand mixer, beat until the butter is fluffy.

3. Add the milk, egg, and vanilla to the butter mixture and beat well.

4. Now add the flour in small portions, beating well as you add the flour.

5. Remove the dough from the bowl and shape it into a large ball. Lightly flour, then wrap it in plastic wrap. Refrigerate for at least 1 hour.

6. Preheat the oven to 350°F.

7. Lightly flour a work surface. Roll out the dough with a rolling pin by placing the rolling pin in the middle of the dough and rolling it forward once and backward once. Then flip the dough, turn it 90 degrees, and roll again. Repeat this process until the dough is approximately ⅛-inch thick.

8. Use a person- or skeleton-shaped cookie cutter to cut out your cookies. Then, take the dough scraps, form it in a ball, and roll it out again. Repeat this process until you cannot make any more cookies.

9. Place the cookies on parchment paper–covered baking sheets. Freeze for approximately 10 minutes.

10. Bake the cookies for 8 to 10 minutes.

BROWN BUTTER
BOOOOOOK BLONDIES

))》◑◖◖（《 ‒

There are a few things every good spellbook needs—a medieval-looking font, iambic pentameter, and at least one spell for turning a human into an animal. The truly great spellbooks need more—the most powerful and evil spells written in the Devil's own hand, and perhaps a human body part or two built right into the binding.

These spellbooks have none of that, but they will truly delight instead of positively terrify. And the brown butter aroma is sure to help this treat make itself known anywhere in your home.

2 sticks (16 tablespoons) unsalted butter
1½ cups packed dark brown sugar
¼ cup granulated sugar
2 large eggs
2 teaspoons vanilla extract
1¾ cups all-purpose flour

2 teaspoons baking powder
1 teaspoon kosher salt
1 cup chocolate chips
1½ to 2 cups mix-ins such as chocolate chips or crushed pretzels (optional)
16 white chocolate Kisses

1. Place the butter in a small saucepan. Cook over medium heat. When the butter begins to foam, use a teaspoon and skim the foam off the top of the butter into a small bowl. (This will prevent the butter from burning.)

2. Continue to heat the butter without the foam until it becomes fragrant and golden brown, about 10 minutes. There will be brown bits at the bottom of the pan. Remove from the heat and cool to room temperature.

3. While the butter cools, preheat the oven to 350°F, and chop any mix-ins.

4. When the butter is cool, beat together with the brown and granulated sugars on a low speed until just incorporated.

5. Add the eggs and vanilla, and beat until light and fluffy (about 3 minutes). Add flour, baking powder, and salt, and beat on medium speed until mixed.

6. Mix in the chocolate chips with a spatula. If you wish to use mix-ins, fold them in now.

7. Spoon the batter into a greased or lined 9 x 13-inch pan and spread evenly. Bake on the middle rack at 350°F until golden brown and shiny, about 22 to 25 minutes. Remove from the oven and let cool.

8. Once the blondies are cool, cut them into approximately 16 pieces.

9. Remove the Kisses from their wrappers. Plunge 1 Kiss point down into the top of each blondie.

10. Place a chocolate morsel on top of the Kiss in the middle. Put the blondies back in the oven for 2 to 4 minutes until the chocolate is lightly melted. Plate and serve or store in an airtight container for up to 4 days.

MOTHER'S SCORPION PIE

Was ever there as venerated a witch as Mummy? I should think not. And nothing brings more joy to a tired witch than the memory of childhood days eating Mother's scorpion pie. After a long day of learning spells at her skirts, back when you were a mere sprig of a girl, this recipe was a true comfort.

If you're in need of a nostalgic recipe as well, I think you'll enjoy this devilishly delicious pie.

SERVES: 8 | PREP TIME: 20 MINUTES | COOK TIME: 75 MINUTES

1 pie crust (page 127) or store-bought pie crust

2 cups pecans

3 large eggs

4 tablespoons unsalted butter

½ cup brown sugar

1 cup corn syrup

1 tablespoon molasses (unsulfured)

2 teaspoons vanilla extract

½ teaspoon salt

1. Freeze the crust in a pie plate.

2. Preheat the oven to 350°F.

3. Cut a few pecans in half and set them aside. Finely chop the remaining pecans.

4. Beat the eggs in a small bowl.

5. Melt the butter in a saucepan on the stove over low heat.

6. Combine the eggs, butter, brown sugar, corn syrup, molasses, vanilla, and salt in a large bowl, and mix it until completely blended.

7. Remove the pie shell from the oven and sprinkle the chopped pecans on the bottom of the shell.

8. Pour the filling over the chopped pecans.

9. Place the halved pecans on the top of the filling. You can arrange them decoratively, but submerge them under the filling and allow them to rise to the surface while baking.

10. Bake for 30 minutes.

11. Remove the pie from the oven and cover it with aluminum foil so the shell and pecans do not burn. Then bake for another 30 to 45 minutes.

12. Remove the pie from the oven and set it out to cool.

RED VELVET TOMBSTONE CAKE

Did you know that *hallowed* means "sacred," or "consecrated"? It comes from *hallow*, which in turn comes from the Middle English *halowen*. Most church cemeteries have been consecrated so they are, in fact, hallowed ground.

This tombstone cake, on the other hand, has not been blessed, so it won't turn any witches to stone, but it will make your mouth water. If you don't like cream cheese frosting, a simple buttercream will work just as well.

1 cup unsalted butter, softened
1 cup granulated sugar
2 large eggs
1 teaspoon vanilla extract
2½ cups all-purpose flour
¼ cup Dutch-processed cocoa powder

1 teaspoon baking soda
1 teaspoon kosher salt
1 cup buttermilk
1 tablespoon distilled white vinegar
2 tablespoons red food coloring
Cream Cheese Frosting (see below)

1. Preheat the oven to 350°F. Grease two 9-inch round cake pans or coat with cooking spray.

2. In a large bowl, beat together the butter and sugar until light and fluffy (2 or 3 minutes). Add the eggs one at a time, beating well after each. Mix in the vanilla extract.

3. In a separate large bowl, stir together the flour, cocoa, baking soda, and salt. Add half of the dry ingredients to the wet ingredients, mixing until just combined.

4. Add the buttermilk, vinegar, and food coloring, beating well to combine. Add the remaining dry ingredients, folding in until just incorporated.

5. Pour the batter evenly into the two cake pans. Bake about 25 to 30 minutes, until a toothpick inserted into the center comes out clean. Let cool fully before frosting.

CREAM CHEESE FROSTING

2 (8-ounce) blocks of cream cheese, softened
½ cup (1 stick) unsalted butter, softened
4 cups powdered sugar, divided

1 teaspoon vanilla extract
¼ teaspoon kosher salt

1. In a large bowl, beat the cream cheese and butter together until smooth. Add 1 cup of powdered sugar and beat until light and fluffy.

2. Add the vanilla and salt and mix until combined. Add the remaining powdered sugar a ½ cup at a time until the frosting is thick and spreadable.

DELICIOUS SPIDER CUPCAKES

Now *these* are pretty spiders, perfect for an on-the-go snack! Okay, maybe if you're spending your evening running after three little rat-faced kids, these cupcakes aren't the way to go. But if you're feeling snacky and have a little extra time to decorate baked goods, these are a frighteningly festive treat!

SERVES: 12 | PREP TIME: 20 MINUTES | COOK TIME: 25 MINUTES

4 tablespoons unsalted butter

¼ cup vegetable oil

½ cup water

1 cup all-purpose flour

1 cup granulated sugar

¼ cup plus 2 tablespoons unsweetened cocoa powder

¾ teaspoon baking soda

⅛ teaspoon salt

1 large egg at room temperature

¼ cup buttermilk

1 teaspoon vanilla extract

Chocolate Buttercream (page 51) or Gray Vanilla Frosting (page 140)

spider decorations (licorice for legs, chocolate chips for eyes, chocolate sprinkles, etc.)

1. Preheat the oven to 350°F and line a muffin tin with 12 cupcake liners.

2. Melt the butter in a medium saucepan over low heat and add the vegetable oil and water.

3. Sift together the flour, sugar, cocoa powder, baking soda, and salt in a large bowl. Add the melted butter mixture and beat together with a hand mixer on low until smooth.

4. Add the egg and beat until well incorporated, then add the buttermilk and vanilla and beat until smooth. Make sure to scrape the sides of the bowl so that all ingredients are incorporated.

5. Pour or spoon the batter into the liners and bake for about 25 minutes, or until a toothpick inserted in the center of a cupcake comes out clean. Let the cupcakes cool on a baking rack completely before frosting and decorating.

6. Frost the cupcakes using a thin metal spatula or piping bag. Add your desired decorations for spidery spook.

WILLIAM'S WORMY BED DIRT CAKE

Poor zombie boyfriend, he really gets the short end of the stick. He seems like a nice guy, but is so misunderstood for so long. Though, I suppose if you run after a gaggle of children, even if you don't intend to harm them, they might get the wrong idea, particularly when you could have just stayed cozy in your coffin until the magic that woke you wears off. But then, if you've been dead for more than 300 years, your brain and logical reasoning may be a bit fuzzy.

Much like *Hocus Pocus* itself, dirt cake is a '90s classic. Feel free to add gummy worms, creepy candies, or zombie bits to ghoul it up and make a wormy death bed worthy of a benign bogeyman.

SERVES: 10 | PREP TIME: 15 MINUTES, PLUS 30 MINUTES TO CHILL

2 cups cold 2% milk
1 box chocolate pudding mix powder
8 ounces whipped topping

1 bag gummy worms
16 chocolate sandwich cookies

1. Blend the milk and chocolate pudding powder in a bowl with a wire whisk.

2. Add the whipped topping and mix until well blended.

3. Scoop the pudding mixture into individual cups.

4. Add the gummy worms to the pudding cups so that they are mostly submerged, leaving enough remaining gummy worms to garnish.

5. Put chocolate sandwich cookies in a resealable plastic storage bag and crush well with a mallet.

6. Cover the tops of the pudding cups with the crushed chocolate sandwich cookies.

7. Garnish with the remaining gummy worms so it appears they are wiggling their way through the chocolate cookie crumbs.

8. Place the cups on a tray and cover with plastic wrap.

9. Refrigerate for at least 30 minutes.

CHOCOLATE-COVERED FINGER OF A MAN NAMED CLARK

You're probably thinking, why would this spellbook give us a recipe for candy? While Clark Bars are no longer common, they are infinitely more delicious than a chocolate-coated digit.

The exact texture of a Clark Bar's crispy peanut butter center is difficult to "master" but this recipe gives you a similar experience with much less effort. So you can conserve all your strength for trying to outlive the dawn.

SERVES: 15 | PREP TIME: 10 MINUTES |
COOK TIME: 10 MINUTES, PLUS 4 HOURS TO CHILL

1 (14.4-ounce) box graham crackers
2 cups powdered sugar
1 cup (2 sticks) salted butter at room temperature

2½ cups crunchy peanut butter
¼ teaspoon vanilla extract
1 (12-ounce) bag chocolate chips

1. Place the whole graham crackers in a resealable plastic storage bag and gently crush them with a mallet, leaving some medium-sized pieces of crackers.

2. Grease a 9 x 13-inch glass baking pan.

3. Add the graham crackers, powdered sugar, butter, peanut butter, and vanilla extract to a large mixing bowl.

4. Blend the ingredients with a rubber spatula.

5. Press the graham cracker mixture into the baking pan.

6. Using a double boiler, heat the chocolate chips until they are melted. Alternatively, you can melt the chips in the microwave using a microwave-safe glass bowl. Microwave on high for 30-second bursts, stirring well between each, until the chocolate is completely melted.

7. Pour the chocolate evenly over the graham cracker mixture.

8. Cover and place in the fridge for 4 hours.

9. When completely chilled, cut into sections 1 to 1½ inches wide in the shape of a candy bar.

PECAN SANDIE SISTAAAHS!!

These cookies are sure to put a spell on you. Pecan sandies are just as easy to make as they are tasty to eat. But watch out (watch out, watch out, watch out, watch out), these are so delicious you'll probably want to eat them three at a time. If you don't believe me...well, let's just say, I ain't lyin'.

MAKES: ABOUT 6 DOZEN | PREP TIME: 20 MINUTES, PLUS 1 HOUR TO CHILL | COOK TIME: 18 TO 20 MINUTES

⅓ cup finely chopped pecans
1 cup unsalted butter, softened
½ cup granulated sugar

2½ cups all-purpose flour
1 teaspoon vanilla extract

1. Add the pecans to a heavy skillet or sauce-pan and lightly toast over medium heat for 5 to 7 minutes. Stir frequently until the nuts begin to brown and release their oils, then stir constantly until they're a light brown. Remove from the heat and let cool.

2. In a large mixing bowl, beat the butter and sugar with an electric mixer on medium speed until fluffy, about 3 minutes. Gradually add in the flour, beating after adding each portion until just blended. Stir in the pecans and vanilla by hand.

3. Divide the dough in half, and then in half again, and shape each portion into a log about 1½ inches wide. Wrap them in parchment paper or plastic wrap and refrigerate until firm, about 1 hour.

4. Preheat the oven to 325°F. Unwrap the dough and cut into slices about ¼-inch thick. Place the slices about ½ inch apart on greased baking sheets or baking sheets lined with parchment paper.

5. Bake for 18 to 20 minutes to a light golden brown. Let cool for 5 minutes, then transfer the cookies to cooling racks. Finish cooling to room temperature.

Bewitching Brews and Beverages

OIL OF BOIL COCKTAIL

Any witch worth her salt needs a full arsenal of spells and potion ingredients at the ready. You never know when you may need to whip up a magical solution on the fly, or remember a complicated potion from hundreds of years ago. In terms of a witch's starter pack, you can't beat oil of boil—versatile, and much easier to procure than say, a fresh dead man's toe—it can serve as the basis for numerous spells.

This Oil of Boil Cocktail, on the other hand, is a bit more niche. Traditionally called a "Slick Rick," it's not common on a bartender's request list, but it's a unique twist and a lot of fun.

SERVES: 1 | PREP TIME: 5 MINUTES

2 ounces gin
½ ounce lemon juice
½ ounce extra-virgin olive oil

½ ounce simple syrup
1 egg white
pinch of sea salt

1. Chill a coupe glass in the freezer.

2. Fill a cocktail shaker with ice.

3. Add the gin, lemon juice, olive oil, simple syrup, egg white, and sea salt.

4. Shake vigorously and pour into the coupe glass.

NEWT SALIVA

Much like the oil of boil, newt saliva comes in quite handy for brewing trouble, summoning mayhem, or just conjuring a bunch of hocus pocus. But bubble, bubble, this one's trouble—there's no downplaying the power of this little potion. Keep an eye on your sparkling wine measurements or you might want a talisman—or ibuprofen—to ward off its evil eye.

SERVES: 1 | PREP TIME: 5 MINUTES

¾ ounce triple sec
¼ ounce lemon juice
1 egg white

dash maraschino liqueur
4 ounces sparkling wine
maraschino cherry

1. Fill a cocktail shaker with ice and pour in the triple sec, lemon juice, egg white, and maraschino liqueur.

2. Shake vigorously so that it is well blended and foamy.

3. Strain into a cocktail glass and top off with sparkling wine.

4. Garnish with a cherry.

"GHOST OF JIMI" HENDRICK'S G&T

Unless you're new in town, you know that All Hallows' Eve is the one night of the year that the spirits of the dead can return to Earth. A chilling thought for those mortal among us. In case the ghost of Jimi Hendrix shows up, pass on the virgin and make this extra-strength Hendrick's Gin & Tonic. A couple of these and you're sure to sleep like the dead.

SERVES: 1 | PREP TIME: 3 MINUTES

2 ounces Hendrick's gin
4 ounces chilled tonic water

1 to 2 lime wedges
1 lime twist

1. Pour the gin and tonic water into a rocks glass filled with ice and stir.

2. Squeeze the lime wedges into the cocktail.

3. Cut the lime twist. Light a match, hold it over the gin and tonic with the pith facing away from the cocktail, and squeeze it into the cocktail so the citrus acid hits the flame and sparks.

4. Quickly run the peel through the flame and then drop the twist into the cocktail.

BLACK FLAME COCKTAIL

I know what you're thinking—you're too cool for school and not afraid of a little old cocktail. But be ye warned—just like black magic and three ancient hags, this cocktail is not to be trifled with. Though it does not include the fat of a hangman, this combination of ingredients could be called hair-raising. So be sure you don't have too many, or thou wouldst hate thyself in the morning.

SERVES: 1 | PREP TIME: 10 MINUTES

⅛ cup sugar
food coloring
lime wedge
2 ounces Captain Morgan Black Rum

½ ounce dry vermouth
blackberry, for garnish
¼ ounce Bacardi 151

1. Chill a cocktail glass.

2. Pour the sugar into a small resealable storage bag.

3. Add a few drops of the food coloring to turn the sugar the desired color. Shake the bag well to distribute the coloring throughout the sugar.

4. Dump the bag contents onto a plate.

5. Use a lime wedge to rim the cocktail glass.

6. Dip the rim of the glass in the colored sugar so it is evenly coated with the sugar.

7. Fill a cocktail shaker with ice. Add the black rum and vermouth and shake well.

8. Strain the cocktail into the rimmed glass.

9. Garnish with a blackberry.

10. Optional: Drizzle the Bacardi 151 onto the top of the cocktail and light on fire. Let it burn out before you drink!

BURNING RAIN OF DEATH PUNCH

))))◑€€€⸱

Much like a modern sprinkler system to a 17th-century witch, this punch *should* send you running for cover. But also like a sprinkler system raining water, you'll find this punch most refreshing. You can use just about any red wine you like, just make sure it is dry (a sweet wine will be too overpowering with the sugar and fruit).

SERVES: 8 | PREP TIME: 5 MINUTES, PLUS 1 HOUR TO CHILL

1 bottle of red wine (merlot or shiraz)

1 cup orange juice

½ cup brandy

12 ounces seltzer

¼ cup granulated sugar

1 orange, sliced

1 red apple, sliced

1 cup blueberries

1 cup strawberries, sliced

1. Pour the bottle of wine, orange juice, brandy, seltzer, and granulated sugar into a large pitcher. Stir until the sugar is dissolved.

2. Stir in the sliced fruit and blueberries.

3. Refrigerate for at least 1 hour.

4. Pour into wineglasses and garnish with an orange slice.

CIRCLE OF SALT MARGARITA

Historically, margaritas have not been the drink to ward *away* ex-boyfriends, but the salt rim on this delicious frozen cocktail should do the trick for any unwanted attention, whether it comes from an ex or a coven of 300-year-old witches.

SERVES: 1 | PREP TIME: 2 MINUTES

coarse salt

2 ounces tequila

1 ounce Cointreau

1 ounce fresh-squeezed lime juice

½ ounce agave syrup

lime wedge

1. Cut a small slit in the lime wedge and rub it around the edge of a chilled margarita glass.

2. Pour a circle of coarse salt and then rim the glass with the salt.

3. Fill half a cocktail shaker with ice.

4. Add the tequila, Cointreau, lime juice, and agave syrup.

5. Shake vigorously and strain into the margarita glass. Garnish with lime wedge.

WITCH'S BREW ESPRESSO MARTINI

While a witch's brew is a pretty generic term when it comes to spellmaking, this recipe is a very specific take. This concoction doesn't bubble, bubble (unless you're using a moka pot), but it does brew up a marvelously magical martini. It leaves only one question—this witch's brew, what's it gonna do to you?

SERVES: 1 | PREP TIME: 22 MINUTES

1½ ounces espresso

1 ounce vodka

1 teaspoon simple syrup

1 ounce heavy cream

1. Brew espresso and let it sit for 20 minutes to cool.

2. Pour the espresso over ice in a rocks glass and give it a stir to cool it further.

3. Add vodka and simple syrup.

4. Add the heavy cream and stir well.

BLOODY MARY'S PICK-ME-UP

The Bloody Mary is a workhorse drink and doesn't need to be reserved just for brunch. That said, a morning Bloody Mary can really work wonders if you were out dancing 'til dawn or if you feel like you've been dead for 300 years—it just might bring you back to life.

SERVES: 1 | PREP TIME: 5 MINUTES

2 ounces vodka

4 ounces tomato juice

dash of Worcestershire sauce

dash of hot sauce (such as Tabasco)

½ teaspoon horseradish

⅛ teaspoon freshly ground pepper

1½ teaspoons lime juice

1 tablespoon lemon juice

1 celery stalk (with leaves), for garnish

1. Add all of the ingredients except the celery stalk to a shaker filled with ice. Stir and strain into a tall glass.

2. Add the celery stalk, to garnish, and serve.

Way to Go
Virgin Drinks

HEALTH-CONSCIOUS LA SMOOTHIE

If you stay away from cigarettes, cycle to school every day, and avoid anyone looking to suck out your life force, you should be able to live to a relatively healthy old age. Perhaps not forever, but a respectable number. Incorporating fruits and veggies through this health-conscious smoothie won't hurt either. Now that's truly tubular.

SERVES: 4 | PREP TIME: 5 MINUTES | COOK TIME: 5 MINUTES

2 kiwis

1 banana

1 pear

2 cups almond milk

14 ounces frozen fruit (mango, pineapple, strawberry)

2 ounces fresh spinach or kale

1. Slice the kiwis, banana, and pear, and add to the blender.

2. Add the rest of the ingredients and blend them well.

3. Pour the blended smoothie in a glass to enjoy.

4. Divide the remaining smoothie into 8-ounce mason jars, but do not fill.

5. Place the mason jars in the freezer to store as leftovers.

AIRHEAD VIRGIN MOCKTAIL

Do you ever just feel like the world is full of airheads and you're the only thing keeping people from causing their own doom? Okay, that may be a touch dramatic, but many of us can relate to dedicating a lot of energy to something, only to have one single thing (or overconfident teenager) mess it up for us all. If you feel me, you might enjoy this snidely named beverage. This drink is suitable for minors—it's a virgin beverage, after all—but if you're between 21 and 300 years of age, feel free to add a bit of your favorite whiskey to stiffen it up.

SERVES: 1 | PREP TIME: 5 MINUTES

1 Braeburn apple, sliced into eighths

ice

1 teaspoon ground cinnamon

½ teaspoon turbinado sugar

1 tablespoon lemon juice

1 cup sparkling water

1 fresh rosemary sprig

1 cinnamon stick

1. Muddle one of the apple slices in the bottom of a tall glass.

2. Add the ice, cinnamon, and sugar.

3. Pour the lemon juice and sparkling water over the ice.

4. Garnish with the rosemary sprig, cinnamon stick, and an apple slice.

SOUL-WARMING HOT CHOCOLATE

A brush with the undead, a most dire and stressful evening, seeing your parents dancing in public—any number of sinister or grim events might chill your blood when the full moon is out and ancient magic's in the air. If your hand, heart, or soul could use a little warming, try this delicious hot chocolate recipe. It will take you back to your innocent, impish youth.

SERVES: 2 | PREP TIME: 2 MINUTES | COOK TIME: 10 MINUTES

2 cups unsweetened almond milk (or 2% milk)

5 teaspoons unsweetened cocoa powder

⅛ teaspoon maple syrup

1 ounce amaretto (optional)

1. Add the milk and cocoa powder to a saucepan over medium heat.

2. When warm, but before boiling, add the maple syrup.

3. Stir with a whisk until boiling.

4. Once boiling, simmer for 5 minutes.

5. Pour the amaretto into two mugs, if using.

6. Pour hot chocolate into the mug.

PEACH SUNRISE MOCKTAIL

There's nothing like watching the sun rise—particularly when it marks the end of an epic night-long battle against three she-devils. This Peach Sunrise Mocktail is the perfect way to toast the end of a dark night (or a long day).

If your adversaries can't be vanquished by the crack of dawn and you need something stronger for your troubles, add your favorite alcohol (a clear alcohol may work better with these flavors than a brown).

SERVES: 1 | PREP TIME: 2 MINUTES

3 ounces peach juice (or nectar)

1 ounce cranberry juice

4 ounces lemon-lime soda

dash of grenadine

fresh mint leaf, for garnish

1. Pour the peach juice, cranberry juice, and lemon-lime soda over ice in a tall glass. Stir well.

2. Add a dash of grenadine and let it slowly drip to the bottom of the glass.

3. Garnish with a mint leaf and serve.

PARENTS' PARTY SPICED APPLE CIDER

Rich-people Halloween parties are so lame, but when they give out the best candy on the block, they're a definite must-visit. Try to get out of bobbing for apples, and keep your visit to a quick glass of this warm apple cider and a Chocolate Witch Pop (see page 52).

This cider is good both spiced and spiked—just add your favorite whiskey, rye, or bourbon.

SERVES: 8 | PREP TIME: 10 MINUTES | COOK TIME: 2½ HOURS

4 Red Delicious or Gala apples
3 Granny Smith apples
3 Golden Delicious apples
1 orange
5 cinnamon sticks

¾ tablespoon ground nutmeg
2½ teaspoons whole cloves
12 cups water
⅔ cup brown sugar
1 ounce spiced rum

1. Slice the apples and orange into twelfths and remove the cores.

2. Place the apple slices, orange slices, and cinnamon sticks in a large pot, preferably a cast-iron Dutch oven.

3. Add the ground nutmeg and whole cloves.

4. Add the 12 cups of water, or enough water to cover the ingredients and fill the pot.

5. Heat the water uncovered over medium heat until it simmers. Reduce the heat and let it sit for 1 hour.

6. Use a potato masher to mash the apple slices and orange slices.

7. Let the water and fruit simmer for at least another hour. The water level will reduce by about an inch.

8. Ladle the ingredients into another pot through a strainer, regularly pressing the apple mash with the bottom of the ladle to get all of the excess cider out of the apple mash.

9. Restrain the cider until the desired amount of pulp is removed.

10. Add the brown sugar and whisk until blended.

11. Pour into a mug over the spiced rum and garnish with a cinnamon stick.

12. Pour the remaining cider into a mason jar and chill.

Odds and Ends

PIE CRUST

This pie crust recipe is easy to master and will frequently come in handy in the kitchen. Use it for savory pies with baked children or chicken (Chicken Pot Pie on page 22), or dessert pies like Mother's Scorpion Pie (page 84) or Pumpkin Pie (page 37).

MAKES: 2 PIE CRUSTS | PREP TIME: 15 MINUTES | CHILL TIME: 2+ HOURS

2½ cups all-purpose flour

1 teaspoon salt

6 tablespoons unsalted butter, chilled and cubed

¾ cup vegetable shortening, chilled

½ cup ice-cold water

1. In a large bowl mix together the flour and salt. Add the butter and shortening and cut together using a pastry cutter until it forms small pebbles.

2. Drizzle in the cold water, 1 tablespoon at a time, stirring with a wooden spoon. Stop adding water when the mixture begins forming large clumps.

3. Transfer the mixture to a floured work surface and lightly knead (with floured hands) until the dough is fully incorporated. The dough should not feel sticky.

4. Form the dough into two equal balls. Flatten each half into a disc about 1-inch thick. Wrap tightly in plastic wrap and refrigerate for at least 2 hours.

5. When you roll out the dough for your recipe, do so on a cold and lightly floured surface. Roll from the center out using gentle but firm pressure.

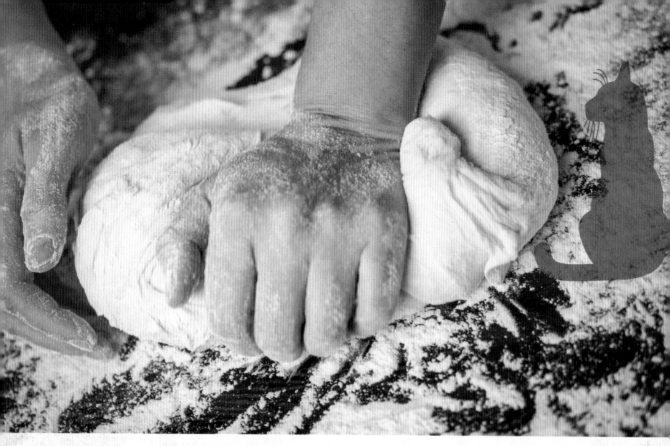

HOMEMADE PASTA

Homemade pasta often sounds like it promises to be most dire and stressful, but once you try it, you'll see it really can be easier than riding a broom.

MAKES: ABOUT 1 POUND (6 SERVINGS) | PREP TIME: 1½ HOURS | COOK TIME: 3 MINUTES

1 cup 00 flour
1 cup semolina flour
pinch of salt

3 large eggs
5 large egg yolks
1 tablespoon olive oil

1. Pour both flours on a clean countertop into a neat pile and sprinkle a pinch of salt on top.

2. Use a fork to quickly blend flours and salt together. Then, with the fork, move most of the flour into a circular ridge, with just a small portion (a few tablespoons) in the center of the ridge.

3. Crack the 3 eggs into a large bowl.

4. Separate the yolks from the 5 eggs and add the yolks to the bowl.

5. Add the olive oil to the eggs and beat with a fork.

6. Pour the eggs into the center of the crater.

7. Using a fork, start combining the eggs with the flour by pulling portions of the flour from the ridge into the center and whipping it with the eggs. Continue to do this until a dough forms that is firm enough for you to start kneading it with your hands.

8. Once the dough is ready to be kneaded, knead the dough by folding it in half and rolling it forward in a motion that pushes the top half into the fold. Then repeat this motion in the other diagonal direction. As you are doing this, continue to sprinkle flour on the countertop to keep the dough from sticking to the counter.

9. Continue to knead the dough until it is no longer sticky to the touch. To test its readiness to sit, form the dough into a ball and gently push down on it in the center with your thumb. If the thumb imprint bounces back into shape, the dough is done being kneaded.

10. Cover the dough in plastic wrap sprinkled with flour and let it sit on the counter for at least 30 minutes.

11. Unwrap the dough and cut it into four pieces.

12. Select a section of dough and sprinkle it and the counter with flour.

13. Roll the dough out with a rolling pin by placing the rolling pin in the center of the dough and rolling it forward once and backward once. Flip the dough upside down, turn it 9 degrees, and roll it again. Continue to roll out the dough, adding flour to the counter as needed, until it is thin enough that you can see your hand through when you lift it from underneath.

14. Use a large knife (or preferably a dough cutter) to cut your pasta into spaghetti, ravioli, pappardelle, or whatever shape you want.

15. Wrap the scraps lightly sprinkled with flour and set them aside.

16. Repeat this for the remaining ¾ of dough. Then combine the scraps and, if not too stiff, try to roll out the scraps to get another sheet of pasta.

17. Hang the pasta sheets on a pasta tree, or gently and loosely fold it and let it sit out for at least 30 minutes.

18. Bring a large pot of salted water to a boil and add the pasta.

19. Cook the pasta for approximately 3 minutes stirring constantly. (You may want to have a small piece of the pasta, separate from the sheets in the water, so you can taste a small piece to test if it is cooked.)

20. Drain the pasta.

GARLIC PARMESAN DIPPING SAUCE

This creamy garlic dipping sauce is a tasty addition to the children's—I mean, chicken—wings on page 64. The creamy parmesan cools the spice of the Old Bay seasoning quite marvelously.

MAKES: 1 CUP | PREP TIME: 10 MINUTES

½ cup mayonnaise
½ cup sour cream
2 cloves garlic, diced
⅓ cup freshly grated parmesan cheese

2 tablespoons fresh chopped Italian parsley
2 tablespoons white vinegar
sea salt
freshly ground pepper

1. Mix the mayonnaise and sour cream in a medium mixing bowl.

2. Add the garlic, parmesan cheese, parsley, white vinegar, salt, and pepper and mix well.

PICO DE GALLO

This fast and easy pico de gallo is a perfect complement to the Hearty Breakfast Frittata on page 13, or any number of other dishes. You can mix up the proportions to your taste. If, for instance, you like a milder salsa, cut down on the jalapeno.

SERVES: 4 | PREP TIME: 10 MINUTES

3 cups grape tomatoes, diced
½ jalapeno, seeded and diced
½ medium red onion, diced
1 small bunch cilantro, finely chopped

3 cloves garlic, diced
juice of ½ lime
sea salt
freshly ground pepper

1. Toss the tomatoes, jalapeno, onion, cilantro, garlic, and lime juice in a medium bowl.

2. Add the sea salt and pepper to taste.

WHIPPED CREAM

Homemade whipped cream isn't a necessity, but it certainly adds a little something extra to any dessert, like Mother's Scorpion Pie on page 84 or the Soul-Warming Hot Chocolate on page 119. Plus, it's a snap to whip up, easier than riding a broom—and certainly easier than negotiating a Hoover.

MAKES: 1 BATCH | PREP TIME: 5 MINUTES

2 cups cold heavy whipping cream
¼ cup powdered sugar

2 teaspoons vanilla extract

1. Place a metal bowl or the bowl of your stand mixer in the freezer for 20 minutes.

2. Set up your stand or electric mixer with the whisk attachment and chilled metal mixing bowl.

3. Add the cold heavy whipping cream, powdered sugar, and vanilla extract to the bowl.

4. Whip on high and watch closely. Turn off the mixer quickly when the whisk or beater turns and causes small peaks to form in the cream. If mixing by hand, whisk constantly and vigorously until peaks form, approximately 5 minutes.

5. Use immediately, or cover the bowl and keep the cream chilled in the refrigerator for up to a day.

BUBBLE, BUBBLE BOURBON CARAMEL SAUCE

This thick and gooey bourbon caramel sauce is a star in its own right but is the perfect complement to the Dump Out Your Chocolate Sack sundae on page 53 or any number of autumnal pies. If you're not a fan of bourbon, just leave it out. But add it in and you'll get a treat so sinfully delicious, the only thing you'll desire more will be....children.

MAKES: ABOUT 3 CUPS | COOK TIME: 15 MINUTES

2 sticks unsalted butter
2 cups brown sugar
1 cup heavy cream
¼ teaspoon salt

½ teaspoon vanilla extract
⅓ cup bourbon whiskey
(or however much you like, really)

1. Combine the butter, brown sugar, cream, and salt in a medium saucepan. Heat over low-medium heat until everything is melted and combined. Drizzle in the vanilla.

2. Turn up the heat to high until the mixture boils and let it bubble for a minute or two. Then turn down the heat to medium high and let it boil for another 4 to 5 minutes (this will help the mixture thicken).

3. When the caramel is a thickness you like, take the pot off the burner and pour in the bourbon, stirring as you go.

4. Let the mixture cool completely, then store in the refrigerator in an airtight container. It will keep for up to 2 weeks, but be sure not to keep it in the coldest part of the fridge (usually the top) as that will cause the sauce to thicken too much and get a little grainy.

CINNAMON PECAN SYRUP

This syrup is as sweet as a delicious victory over a pack of brats and perfect for drizzling over the Pumpkin Pancakes on page 17.

MAKES: 1 CUP | COOK TIME: 10 MINUTES

½ cup chopped pecans
1 cup maple syrup

1 teaspoon ground cinnamon

1. Warm a small saucepan over medium heat.

2. Add the pecans to the saucepan and let them warm for a few minutes, stirring often, to lightly toast them so they begin to release their oil.

3. Add the maple syrup and cinnamon. Bring to a simmer and let lightly bubble for about a minute.

4. Serve warm or let cool.

GRAY VANILLA FROSTING

This vanilla buttercream recipe is almost easier to make than plucking a juicy spider snack out of a web. You can use this for the Delicious Spider Cupcakes on page 89, or if you're not a fan of cream cheese frosting, this is an easy swap for the Red Velvet Tombstone Cake on page 86.

MAKES: 2 CUPS | PREP TIME: 20 MINUTES

½ cup vegetable shortening
½ cup (1 stick) unsalted butter, softened
1 teaspoon vanilla extract
4 cups sifted powdered sugar

2 tablespoons milk
pinch of salt
gray food coloring

1. Cream together the shortening and butter in a large bowl using a mixer on medium speed until light and fluffy (about 1 or 2 minutes). Beat in the vanilla extract.

2. Add in the powdered sugar about 1 cup at a time, beating thoroughly after each cup. Make sure to scrape the sides of the bowl so that all the sugar is incorporated. Once all the sugar is mixed in, the icing should look stiff.

3. Drizzle in the milk while continuing to mix until the icing reaches the desired consistency, smooth and fluffy. Mix in the pinch of salt and food coloring until the icing is fully colored.

Recipe Index

Acknowledgments

First and foremost, huge thanks (again) to all of my colleagues at Ulysses Press, for continuing to make fantastic books and an excellent workplace. Thank you for caring about '90s Halloween films and campy witchery, especially Casie Vogel (again) and Ashten Evans, who knew how important this project was to me and brought me in on it in the first place. And thanks to Claire, Jake, and Renee for production and editing brilliance.

Thanks of course to Andrew, who taught me pretty much everything I know about cooking except how to make chicken, which I taught him.

Thank you to Emily, Alex, Ann, Bri, Kathryn, Norm, Hattie, Angela, Ben, Megan, Caitlin, and anyone who has ever watched *Hocus Pocus* with me, which was probably only a small handful of people, but over hundreds of viewings.

Huge thanks to Bette, Sarah, and Kathy, who created such delightfully wicked and marvelously quotable characters, and to whoever first thought to give them a big musical number in the middle of the film—your contribution to the arts is forever appreciated.

To Jeff and Reba—thank you for letting me run just a little bit amok as a kid.

And thanks again to Andrew for helping me see that I can when it seems like I can't and making me feel funny even after fourteen years of largely the same jokes. I'm proud of you.

About the Author

Bridget Thoreson is a writer and booklover based in Brooklyn, New York. Her other books include *XOXO: A Cocktail Book* and consulting for *Are You My Wine?* Clearly, Bridget is very interested in drinking, eating, and pop culture.